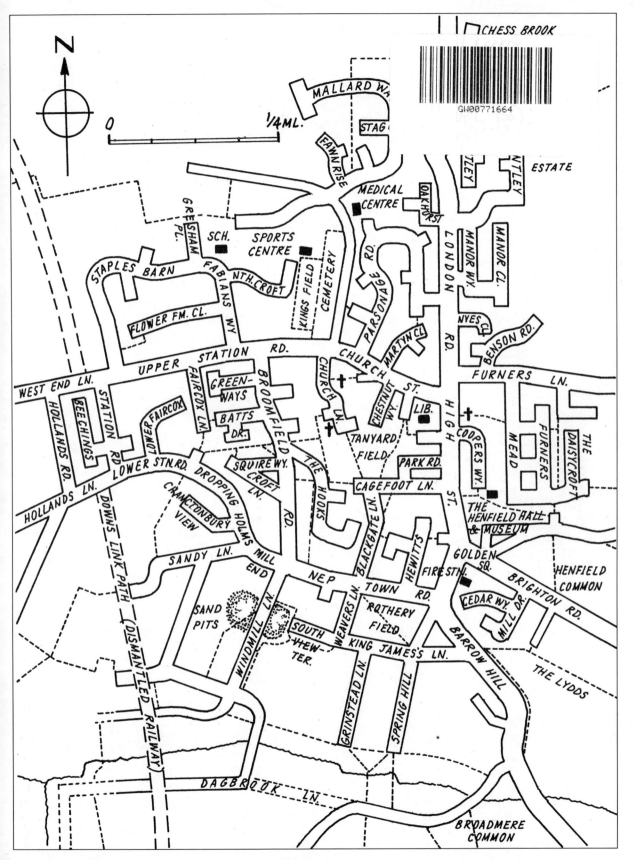

Village street plan.

HENFIELD
A Sussex Village

An aerial view of Henfield looking north in October 1943. The railway line can be seen on the west side of the village, and leading away south the road to Upper Beeding. The market gardens on the southern slopes of the ridge on which the village stands, together with Broadmere Common and Henfield Common are also clearly visible.

HENFIELD
A Sussex Village

Marjorie Carreck & Alan Barwick

edited by Norman Carreck

Phillimore

2002

Published by
PHILLIMORE & CO. LTD,
Shopwyke Manor Barn, Chichester, West Sussex

ISBN 1 86077 210 2

Printed and bound in Great Britain by
BOOKCRAFT LTD
Midsomer Norton, Bath

Contents

	List of Illustrations	vii
	Illustration Acknowledgements	ix
	Acknowledgements	x
One	Henfield's Origins	1
Two	Communications	17
Three	Henfield at Work	31
Four	The Heart of Henfield	57
Five	Henfield at War	77
Six	The People of Henfield	95
Seven	Henfield at Leisure	119
	Bibliography	141
	Index	145

Many of the photographs taken in the 20th century come from the camera of Marjorie Baker. Marjorie was born in Henfield in 1912 and, after being apprenticed to Margaret Ellsmoor from Baker Street, London, she set up as a professional photographer in Henfield in 1932. From her studio in Park Road she has continued to record children, weddings, events, houses, places and people, and provided an invaluable record of Henfield up until 1996. She is seen here photographing a wedding at St Peter's Church in 1965. We thank her for her great support for this project.

List of Illustrations

Frontispiece: Aerial view of Henfield, 1943

1. Map showing geology of the Adur Valley 1
2. Neolithic implements 2
3. Map showing prehistoric finds 3
4. Romano-British silver ring, *c*.550 4
5. Saxon charter of 770 5
6. Artist's impression of Anglo-Saxon settlement 6
7. Entry in Domesday Book, 1086 7
8. St Anthony's Cottage 8
9. Wantley Manor 9
10. Archaeological excavation at Stretham moated site, 1976 9
11. Stretham Manor 10
12. Lashmars Hall 11
13. Barrow Hill farmhouse, *c*.1910 12
14. Chatfields 12
15. Memorial brass to Meneleb Rainsford and Ann Kenwellmersh 13
16. Henfield Place, *c*.1916 14
17. Map of Henfield in *c*.1700 14
18. Henfield High Street, *c*.1870 15
19. South View Terrace, Nep Town 16
20. The village pound and 'shanty' 16
21. *The George Hotel*, 1912 18
22. Dropping Holms before widening 18
23. Broomfield Road, *c*.1914 19
24. Toll charges at High Cross gate 20
25. Tollgate at top of Crouch Hill 21
26. Mock Bridge at Shermanbury 21
27. Outside *The White Hart* 22
28. William Pattenden's coach, *c*.1895 22
29. New Hall in 1948 23
30. Furners Lane, *c*.1912 24
31. Subscriptions towards upkeep of Nep Town Road, *c*.1870 24
32. Location of locks for Baybridge Navigation 25
33. *New Inn*, close to the River Adur 26
34. Henfield railway station 27
35. Henfield station staff, *c*.1920 28
36. Telephone operators, 1960s 30
37. The Pond House, Broadmere Common 32
38. Henfield Brickworks, 1965 33
39. Workmen at Sandy Lane sandpit 33
40. Map of Tanyard in 1844 35
41. Brookside Dairy's delivery cart 36
42. The Henfield workhouse, 2001 37
43. Market gardens in the 1920s 38
44. A Boxing Day shoot, *c*.1913 39
45. Tom Browning's market garden, 1947 39
46. The Violet Nurseries, 1912 40
47. Lavender Cottage, 1921 40
48. Chestham Park 42
49. Henfield Lodge, Woodmancote 42
50. Woods Mill, *c*.1912 43
51. Nep Town windmill, 1885 44
52. Windmill on the Lydds, *c*.1910 44
53. Coopers Yard, before demolition 46
54. Mr Powell outside his shop 46
55. High Street forge, *c*.1917 47
56. Tom Miles in his forge, 1966 48
57. Brazier's garage, 1920s 49
58. High Street looking north, *c*.1890 50

59. Mr Brazier tyring a wheel, c.1910 50
60. Mr Baigent, c.1920 51
61. Vinall's men, c.1900 51
62. Frank Bowler's delivery wagon 52
63. Basket Makers Cottages,
    Broadmere Common 52-53
64. Nep Town Road 54-55
65. Gas Works Cottages, Hollands
    Lane, c.1930 56
66. St Peter's Parish Church, c.1895 57
67. Congregational Church, c.1870 58
68. Nep Town Mission chapel, c.1910 59
69. Rehoboth Baptist chapel, c.1900 60
70. Corpus Christi, 1965 60
71. Clifton House School, c.1866 61
72. Henfield Boys School, c.1910 62
73. Henfield Girls School, c.1912 63
74. Henfield Infants School, 1929 63
75. Library in the Assembly Rooms 64
76. Broomfields, 1971 65
77. Holmwood, 1966 66
78. Nurse Wooller's Cottage,
    Pinchnose Green 67
79. Surgery at Woodlawn, Cagefoot
    Lane 68
80. Election results, 1894 69
81. Lych Gate at Henfield Cemetery,
    c.1890 70
82. Henfield Fire Brigade, c.1910 71
83. Henfield Fire Brigade, 1937 73
84. Henfield's first ambulance, 1935 73
85. Henfield Parish Council, 1965 74
86. Opening of new Village Hall,
    1974 76
87. Lucie Bishop, Henfield Museum 76
88. Parsonage House, c.1914 78
89. The White Hart Inn, c.1885 79
90. Dr C.F. Lewis, c.1890 80
91. Summer camp, c.1910 81
92. Territorial Army, c.1912 82
93. 24th Division Cycle Corps, 1915 83
94. Cheese making, 1918 83
95. Peace Day Procession, 1919 84
96. War Memorial dedication, 1923 85
97. Houses under construction, c.1920 86
98. R.O.C. equipment, 1925 86
99. Home Guard, 1941 87
100. Special constables, 1943 88
101. Decontamination and Rescue Party,
     1944 89
102. V.E. Day, 1945 91
103. Henfield Land Army Club, 1947 91
104. Welcome Home Party, 1948 92
105. Memorial Playing Fields 93
106. 'Prefabs' at Wantley Hill 93
107. Storm damage, 1987 94
108. Woolgar tenements, c.1912 96
109. Thomas Stapleton 97
110. Henry Bysshopp 97
111. Upper Station Road, c.1914 99
112. William Borrer 99
113. Barrow Hill House 100
114. Cedars of Lebanon at Springhills 101
115. Martyn Lodge, c.1870 102
116. Backsettown 103
117. Mockbridge House, c.1912 105
118. Barbara Glasby in her studio 106
119. The Williamsons in their studio 106
120. The studio at Dykes 107
121. Rowland Emett in 1977 108
122. Cruttenden's baker's shop, 1920s 109
123. Musson's grocer's shop, c.1917 110
124. Moore's baker's shop, c.1890 110
125. Thorns butcher's shop, c.1920 111
126. Douglas and Robin Funnell in their
     shop, 1965 112
127. High Street looking north, 1950 113
128. Charles Tobitt 113
129. Mr and Mrs Tyler, 1949 114
130. Handbell ringers, c.1896 115
131. Commercial Buildings, c.1906 116
132. Ron Shepherd, c.1930 117
133. Tanyard Pond, 1940s 117
134. Bill Goacher, 1965 117
135. Henfield postmen, 1963 118
136. Cricket match, c.1912 120
137. Athletic Football Club, 1957 121
138. Quoits pitch, Henfield Common 122

139. Stoolball, Tanyard Field, *c*.1910 123
140. Tennis on Kings Field, *c*.1912 124
141. Bowling Green, Golden Square,
        1935 125
142. Bank Holiday pram race 126
143. Market stall, Cagefoot Lane 127
144. Girls' Friendly Society pageant,
        1934 128
145. Scout field, 1952 128
146. Henfield B.P. Guild 129
147. Brownies, Martyn Lodge, *c*.1928 130

148. Young Farmers' Club, 1948 131
149. The 'Rocket', 1937 132-133
150. Henfield Angling Society, 1930s 134
151. Rainbow Coffee Tavern, *c*.1910 135
152. Henfield W.I. seat, High Street 137
153. Darby and Joan Club, 1950s 138
154. The vicarage, 1936 139
155. May Day celebrations, Henfield
        Common, 1920s 139
156. Carnival float in Vinall's yard 140
157. Coronation procession, 1953 140

Illustration Acknowledgements

Illustrations are from the collections of: Alan Barwick, 1, 3, 4, 6, 13, 16, 17, 19, 22-3, 25, 30, 34, 36, 41, 48, 50, 58-9, 64, 72-3, 78, 81, 88, 96, 107-8, 111, 114, 123, 138, 150-1; Marjorie Carreck, 29; Betty Charman, 74, 132, 144; Robin Funnell, 62; Peter Gander, 61; Henfield Evangelical Free Church, 67; Henfield Museum, 10, 20-1, 24, 26-8, 33, 35, 37, 40, 43-7, 52-7, 60, 63, 66, 68-9, 77, 79, 80, 82-7, 89-91 ,93-5, 97-9, 100-2, 104-5, 109-10, 112, 115, 118, 121-2, 124-5, 129-30, 135,-7, 139-41, 146, 148-9, 152-6; Henfield Women's Institute, 11, 12, 18, 31, 38, 51, 70-1, 75, 103, 106, 113, 116, 119-20, 126-8, 134, 143, 145, 157; Betty Hills, 117; Malcolm Knapp, 49; Roger Knight, 65; the late Harry Matthews, 39, 92; Olive Skilton, 131; M. Baker, 76, 133, 142.

Copyrights of illustrations are owned by: Marjorie Baker, 11, 29, 45, 76, 83, 85, 98-101, 103-6, 116, 120, 127, 133, 142, 148-9, 152; Alan Barwick, 1, 3, 4, 6, 17, 22, 107, 114; Stan Carey, 56, 126, 135; Norman Carreck, 8, 9, 14, 15, 32, 42; Roger Gale, 146; the late J. Marren, 137, 153; The Trustees of Parham House, 110.

All maps and line drawings were drawn by Alan Barwick. Modern photographs were taken by Norman Carreck.

We also thank Roy Gander for photographic assistance.

We have made every effort to trace the copyright of photographs used, but if we have inadvertently failed to credit anybody, please contact us via the publishers.

Acknowledgements

The authors would especially like to thank the following for kindly providing information which has been used in this book: John Andrews; Marjorie Baker; The Worshipful Company of Barber Surgeons, for information about Prosper Rainsford; Val Binstead (St Peter's Church of England School); Annette Blair-Fish; Alan Bridgewater; the late Beryl Carling; Anne Collins; Fr. Mark Elvins, for information about the coat of arms; Bob Farren; Monica Harrison; Martin Hayes (local history librarian, Worthing Library); Arthur Hobbs; Mary Holder; Dr Annabelle Hughes; Ann Jury; the Rev. Peter Kefford and the St Peter's Parochial Church Council for permission to consult the church records; Don Lidbetter; John Mills (archaeologist, West Sussex County Council); John Missen; May Morey; Alison Noble, for information about Woods Mill; Peggy Norman; the late Admiral Sir Geoffrey Oliver, for information about the Assembly Rooms; Tony Payne; Janet Pennington (archivist, Lancing College); Barbara Rhys; David Sayers; Don Scutt; Prof. Mark Seward (University of Bradford), for information about William Borrer; Glen Shields, for information about the Rainsford family; John Sinkins; Frank Skilton; Olive Skilton; Mrs J.M. Sleight; Dr John Squire, for information about Henfield doctors, the Nursing Association, the Dame Elizabeth Gresham Charity and many other matters; Mgr Terence Stonehill; Dick Thorns; Chris Tod (Steyning Museum); Laurie Tooth; Gene Turner; Ian Varley; West Sussex Record Office; Peggy Whiting; David Williams; Marion Woolgar.

We also thank Dick Thorns and Eleanor Jenkins for reading and commenting on the manuscript.

We gratefully thank Henfield Parish Council for allowing the use of photographs, paintings and documents from Henfield Museum. We gratefully thank Henfield Women's Institute for allowing the use of pictures and articles from their volumes of scrapbooks.

Finally we would like to thank May Morey for assistance in many ways.

One

HENFIELD'S ORIGINS

HENFIELD IS AN ANCIENT VILLAGE. History books used to tell how Anglo-Saxon invaders carved settlements and farms out of 'wildwood' upon which pre-historic, Celtic and Roman peoples had made little impression. The books then went on to tell how Norman invaders developed a system of agriculture based on communal open fields and strip cultivation, which in turn was swept away by Georgian enclosures to produce the countryside we know today. Over the last fifty years, however, historians have come to realise that this story is only applicable to certain parts of Britain such as the Midlands, and that other parts, notably much of south-east England, are far more ancient, and may have assumed much of their present appearance long before the Romans saw them. There is ample evidence that Henfield falls into this category.

Henfield lies a few miles north of the South Downs on a ridge of high ground overlooking the River Adur. Its name is of Anglo-Saxon origin from *Hamfelde*, meaning 'dwelling place on high open land'. This ridge, formed from the Lower Greensand rock, was an ideal site for a settlement, with its abundance of springs and a light sandy soil which could be cultivated easily. The Weald Clay to the north and south supported dense woodland. Up until medieval times the River Adur was an arm of the sea covering all of the present water meadows which are known locally as 'the brooks'. The

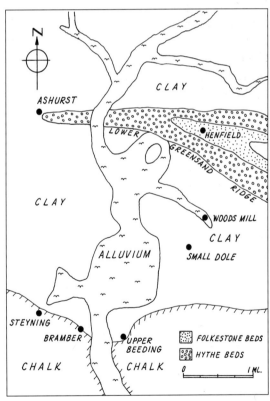

1 Map showing the geology of the lower Adur Valley and the location of Henfield and other settlements.

1

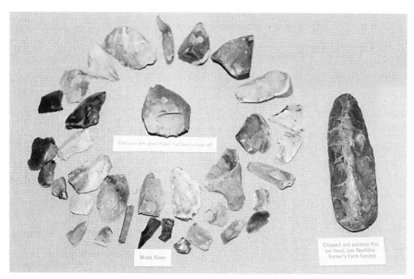

2 A collection of Neolithic implements in Henfield Museum. The earliest settlers used flint from the chalk to make their knives, scrapers, axes and other tools.

name Adur dates only from the 16th century; in the 10th century it was known as 'The Bremre' and in the 13th and 14th centuries as the 'Water of Bramber'.

That the Saxons particularly noted the ridge was 'open' indicates that somebody had already cleared the natural woodland. Who could have done this? The Palaeolithic or Old Stone Age peoples (500,000–10,000 B.C.) used the Greensand ridge as an east-west trackway across southern England. A few traces have been found locally of these nomadic hunter-gatherers, including a palaeolithic axe in Furners Lane. Abundant evidence of the existence of Mesolithic peoples (10,000–3,500 B.C.) has been found at the north-east corner of Henfield Common near the sand pit. Here there was a working floor where tools were made, and a number of flint flake tools and the flint cores from which they originated have been found. Unsubstantiated finds of flint arrowheads have also been made at Rye Farm.

Around 3,500 B.C. Neolithic people from the Mediterranean area colonised the South Downs, and established permanent settlements. They produced pottery, grew cereals, carried out weaving, and kept domesticated animals. A late-Neolithic chipped and polished axe-head has been found in the sand pit north of Henfield Common, and a laurel-leaf flint spear head in the garden of a bungalow to the west of the Rothery Field at Nep Town. The approach road to Henfield from the south climbs 'Barrow Hill', suggesting that this may have been the site of a Neolithic or Bronze-Age burial, but no evidence has been found of this. A map of 1724 calls it 'Barron Hill', suggesting an altogether different origin for the name.

The Bronze Age (2,000-500 B.C.) is associated with peoples who came across the English Channel and tended to colonise the Wealden woodland, setting up isolated farmsteads and the occasional hamlet. They lived in conical huts with a central hearth. Evidence of their existence in Henfield came to light during building work on the corner of Furners Lane and Furners Mead in 1999, when the top of a Bronze-Age burial urn was found.   The Iron Age (500 B.C. onwards) was marked by the settlement of the Weald by Celtic people from across the Channel. They established the local fortified downland settlements at Cissbury, Chanctonbury, Devil's Dyke and Wolstonbury. These forts provided both a centre for trade and a place of refuge in case of attack. In this period flint and bronze tools were replaced by iron ones, and the iron industry established itself in the Weald, which was rich in both iron ore and wood. Improved agricultural techniques resulted in surpluses of grain and wool which could be traded for iron and other commodities.

Surveys have revealed numerous Celtic field boundaries high on the South Downs. Historians have often suggested that these peoples preferred such remote and inhospitable places, but it is surely more reasonable to suppose that people only attempted to farm and live in such extreme locations because the more easily cultivated land was already fully utilised. Definite evidence for Celtic cultivation of the lowlands is less easy to find,

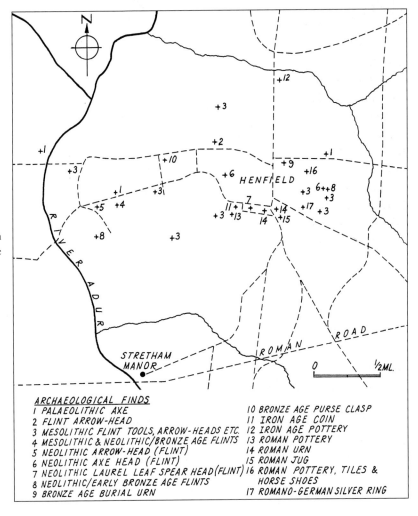

3 Map showing the location of prehistoric finds and the ancient trackways.

ARCHAEOLOGICAL FINDS
1 PALAEOLITHIC AXE
2 FLINT ARROW-HEAD
3 MESOLITHIC FLINT TOOLS, ARROW-HEADS ETC.
4 MESOLITHIC & NEOLITHIC/BRONZE AGE FLINTS
5 NEOLITHIC ARROW-HEAD (FLINT)
6 NEOLITHIC AXE HEAD (FLINT)
7 NEOLITHIC LAUREL LEAF SPEAR HEAD (FLINT)
8 NEOLITHIC/EARLY BRONZE AGE FLINTS
9 BRONZE AGE BURIAL URN
10 BRONZE AGE PURSE CLASP
11 IRON AGE COIN
12 IRON AGE POTTERY
13 ROMAN POTTERY
14 ROMAN URN
15 ROMAN JUG
16 ROMAN POTTERY, TILES & HORSE SHOES
17 ROMANO-GERMAN SILVER RING

4   Silver ring, made in Germany in the Roman style *c.*550, found on Henfield Common in 1979. This demonstrates that people with trading connections with Germany were either living or passing through the area a century after the Roman legions left.

because it will have been obscured by, or mistaken for, later landscape features. Tradition suggests that a faint ditched enclosure standing on the highest point of the ridge north of Henfield Common was an Iron-Age hill-fort, although trial excavations have suggested that it may merely have been a cattle enclosure. An Iron-Age coin has, however, been found in the garden of a house in South View Terrace, a little further west along the ridge.

The Romans invaded Britain in A.D. 43, and their army's occupation lasted nearly 400 years, during which time they built many roads in Sussex, mainly for military purposes. Locally, the Roman 'Greensand Way' crossed the River Adur two miles south of Henfield at a narrow point in its flood plain. It can still be traced on the 1:2500 Ordnance Survey map, cutting across a much older field pattern, and incorporates parts of Horn Lane near to Woods Mill, and parts of the New Hall farm road. The stone road remains under the fields, and ploughs reputedly scrape on its surface.

Roman country life centred around 'villas' with their large estates. Although many are known in Sussex, such as those at Bignor near Chichester, and Danny near Hurstpierpoint, no Roman dwelling site has been positively identified near Henfield. Roman artefacts have, however, been found locally. These include a jug and urns on Barrow Hill, possibly indicating the presence of a cemetery, and pottery, tiles and horse shoes, suggesting a building of some importance, have been found at Backsettown. At Thundersbarrow Hill, on the South Downs five miles south of Henfield, a small Romano-British village has been excavated.

After the Roman legions left in *c.*410 Saxon invaders made their way up the Adur to settle on the dry banks. One such settlement was *Stret-ham*, the 'dwelling place by the street'. The first dwelling house at Stretham would have been made of wood, and nothing remains of it above ground, but just to the north-west of the present 'Downs Link' path its site of approximately one acre can still be seen, bounded by a moat on three sides, next to where the Woods Mill stream enters the river. A Saxon quay has been excavated here, demonstrating the importance of water as a means of transport.

Away from Stretham, on the Greensand ridge at Henfield, a more extensive settlement was developing. In 770 Earl Warbald and his wife Titburh were granted a charter by Osmund, King of Sussex, for 15 hides (approximately 1,800 acres) of land on which to build and support a church dedicated to St Peter, in Henfield. This is the earliest

THE BEGINNING

The Charter of King Osmund

THIS is a facsimile of the earliest known copy of the Charter of Osmund, King of the West Saxons, granted in 770 to Earl Warbald, Lord of the Manor of Stretham, to assign land for the endowment of a Church at Henfield.

It comes from a cartulary — or book of ecclesiastical records — probably made between 1368 and 1385, when William Rede was Bishop of Chichester. It is written in monkish Latin and may well be the last of several successive copies of the original Charter, executed 600 years earlier. The episcopal recorder could copy the Latin, but had to skip a passage written in Saxon.

Here is the translation —

"IN the name of our Lord Jesus Christ ! We have brought nothing into this world, and it is certain we can carry nothing out. Therefore the eternal rewards are to be sought by means of earthly and transitory things. Therefore I, Osmund, having been asked by my venerable Thegn Warbald and his wife Titburh, (to be so good as to grant) them a little land for the Church of St. Peter the Apostle, which is in that spot, I grant in perpetual possession (land) of 15 hides* in the place which is called Henfield, with all things pertaining thereto, that is, fields, woods, pastures, meadows, rivers, springs. This charter was done in the year 770 from the incarnation of our Lord Jesus Christ. *Then follow the bounds or precincts of the aforesaid land in the Saxon tongue.* I, Osmund, King, have signed this gift with my own hand. I, Osa, archbishop, have agreed and signed. I, Hedda, bishop, have agreed and signed. I, Eadberht, bishop, have agreed and signed. I, Offa, freely confirm this charter with the above named persons. I, Wilfrid, bishop, have agreed. I, Brorda, alderman. I, Berhtwald, alderman. I, Eadbald, alderman. I, Esne, alderman. I, Aldwulf, alderman, &c."

With acknowledgements to Mrs. Gill, Diocesan Record Office, Chichester, and to E. Barker, Sussex Archaelogical Collections, Vol. 86, 1947.

* Hide; a portion of land variously estimated as from 60 to 120 acres, originally enough to support a family and its dependants.

ii

5   Copy of the Saxon charter of 770.

documentary evidence for the dedication of a church in Sussex, for it was only in 681 that St Wilfrid had landed at Selsey to convert the South Saxons to Christianity. The original church was probably a wooden structure on the site of the present parish church. Warbald was lord of the manor of Stretham, which included most of the present parish of Henfield. This manor eventually passed to the bishops of Selsey, and remained in the hands of bishops for 1,100 years.

Saxon life revolved around smaller isolated farmsteads and villages. At about the same time as the first Saxon settlement grew up at Stretham, a thriving town and port was developing only two miles downriver at Steyning. This must have had an influence on the smaller settlements at Stretham and Henfield, for Steyning traded with France, and extracted salt from the saltwater of the tidal river in saltpans. Evidence of these can be seen today at Upper Beeding.

By the beginning of the 10th century the Saxons had established a pattern of village settlements, with parish boundaries which were ecclesiastical divisions and which in many cases still remain today. The present parish of Henfield occupies approximately 4,400 acres, indicating that it has grown considerably in size since the first charter was granted. Saxon units of administration and courts of justice were 'hundreds', possibly consisting of a hundred families. In Henfield this was the 'Hundred of Tippa's Oak' or *Tipnoak Hundred* (sometimes referred to just as 'Henfield Hundred'). The meeting place of the hundred court may have been the *Mot-Stow* or Moustows. *Hundred Steddle*, at nearby Woodmancote, probably commemorates some stone or other object which marked the south-eastern boundary of the hundred.

6 An artist's impression of an Anglo-Saxon settlement. The large central building is where people would meet and eat, and around it are smaller buildings where they would sleep, work and store food and materials.

7 The entry for Henfield in
Domesday Book, 1086. A hide
is a measurement of land
(approximately 120 acres), and
a plough indicates a team of
eight oxen. The value of
Henfield in 1086 at £10 can
be compared with nearby
Steyning which, although
today not much larger than
Henfield, was in 1086 an
important town and port,
valued at £100.

In HAMFELDE HVND.

Ipfe eps teñ in dñio *HAFELDE* . T.R.E. fe defd p̄ xv . hid.
7 m̄ p̄ . xɪ . hid 7 una uirgꜩ . Tra . ē . xx . car̄ . In dñio funt . ɪɪ . car̄.
7 xxɪɪɪ . uiłłi cū . xv . bord hn̄t . x . car̄ . Ibi æcc̄la . 7 xʟ . ac̄ p̄ti.
Moliñ 7 pifcaria defuꝴ p̄ fup̄facto . W . de braiofe.
De his hid teñ Wiłłs . . . . de epo . ɪɪɪ . hid . 7 ibi hr̄
in dñio . ɪ . hid . 7 ɪ . uiłłs cū . x . bord hn̄t dim̄ car̄ . Silua
de . ɪɪɪ . porc̄ . Totū m̄ T.R.E. ualeb̄ . x . lib̄ . 7 poft: vɪɪ . lib̄.
Modo qd eps teñ: x . lib̄ . Qd miles teñ: xʟ . fol . 7 tam̄
fuit ad firmā . p̄ xvɪɪɪ . lib̄.
In *LEWES* funt . ɪɪɪ . burḡes ad hoc m̄ p̄tiñtes . redd̄ . xxɪ . den̄.

The Bishop himself holds
in HENFIELD Hundred
2 HENFIELD, in lordship. Before 1066 it answered for 15 hides;
now for 11 hides and 1 virgate. Land for 20 ploughs.
In lordship 2 ploughs.
   23 villagers with 15 smallholders have 10 ploughs.
   A church; meadow, 40 acres. A mill and a fishery are lacking,
      through encroachment by William of Braose.

William [a man-at-arms?] holds 3 of these hides from the Bishop.
He has 1 hide in lordship.
   1 villager with 10 smallholders have ½ plough.
   Woodland at 3 pigs.
Value of the whole manor before 1066 £10; later £7; now,
what the Bishop holds, £10; what the man-at-arms holds, 40s;
however, it was at a revenue for £18.
In Lewes are 3 burgesses who belong to this manor; they pay 21d.

The Norman Conquest in 1066 brought changes. In order to defend the coast, Sussex was divided into six divisions or 'rapes', held by strong Norman nobles, each with a section of coast, a castle, a port, and a strip of land running north to the great Wealden woodland, then known as *Andredsweald*. Henfield was placed in the Rape of Bramber, whose port was moved from Old Shoreham, a Saxon port then becoming silted up, to New Shoreham, the present site further south. The castle was at Bramber, guarding the market town of Steyning, and the rape was controlled by Sir William de Braose. The Manor of Stretham continued, however, to be in the hands of the church rather than de Braose. The bishopric, which had been at isolated Selsey in Saxon times, was moved by the Normans to the thriving city of Chichester, so the new Norman bishop of Chichester became the lord of the manor of Stretham.

Domesday Book of 1086 tells us something of the village in Norman times. Already there had been some division of the manor, as William, a 'man at arms', held land with his own labourers in return for supporting the king in times of war. This land may have been the 'Hall Lands' or *Hollands*, on the western edge of the village. Not all of Henfield was in the Manor of Stretham. To the north-east was the small Manor of Wantley, of about 170 acres, separate from the bishop's land, held by the Norman Ralph de Buci after whom *Kingston Buci* (now Kingston-by-Sea) near Shoreham was named. Two smaller manors, Moustows to the east of the High Street, and Oreham, one mile south-east of Henfield, were also later formed out of the Manor of Stretham.

No buildings are known to survive from the early Norman period. Generations of houses would no doubt have come and gone until more lasting materials were used for their construction. Scattered all over the parish would have been the humble dwellings of the 23 'villeins' and 15 'bordars' who farmed the various parts of the manor. The feudal system which had existed under the Saxons had become more refined under the Normans. 'Villeins' or villagers were semi-free peasants, who as well as working on the land belonging to the lord of the manor would also work their own land consisting of several acres. 'Bordars' were lower down the social scale, having less land, again having to work for the lord, and their dwellings would have been of very simple construction. Houses grew up around the church and probably in the present High Street, where east-west and north-south trackways met, and also at Nep Town.

The bishop's manor house at Stretham must have been rebuilt several times until stone was eventually used for its construction. Excavations in the moated field have revealed a stone building, probably an early manor house with an integral chapel built *c.*1250. This was replaced *c.*1325 by a timber-framed house, which was abandoned as a dwelling altogether by *c.*1350, perhaps due to flooding. During the 13th and 14th centuries the bishops were in residence at Stretham on a number of occasions as they travelled around their diocese, but to the people of Henfield they must have remained shadowy figures, the estate largely being managed by stewards. The present Stretham Manor, on the south-east side of the 'Downs Link' path, is part of a much larger timber-framed house built *c.*1450 on drier ground.

8 St Anthony's Cottage, built *c.*1390. This is the oldest of five 'hall houses' built on the east side of the High Street. It originally had a large open hall with a fire in the centre, the adoption of chimneys not being usual until *c.*1550. Red Barn Cottage next door was a later addition.

9 The rear part of Wantley Manor in the High Street is another 'hall house', built during the 14th century. On the north side of the building is a medieval barn.

10 Archaeological dig in progress at the Stretham moated site in 1976. The photograph shows the stone revetment of one of the buildings close to the river with what may be a garderobe (i.e. lavatory) chute clearly visible.

A 'Custumal of the Manor of Stretham' of 1374 describes in detail the 'customs' and tenants of the manor, and their duties. It describes the bishop's deer park, which could be approached from the parish church via what is now the farm track to the east of the modern cemetery and is commemorated in the road name 'Deer Park' on the new housing estate on the north side of the village. The park remained enclosed until the end of the Civil War, in the late 1640s, by which time much of the fence had been destroyed. In the centre of the park was a hundred acres of woodland, part of which survives today as Parsonage Wood. Another wood held by the bishop was *le Woghwoode*, south of Woods Mill, now known as Hoe Wood. The bishop also had an extensive hunting ground called Goseden Chase to the north of Henfield, which 'extends from Warthynglith [Warninglid] to Wyndeham [Wineham] ... and thence to Mockeford [Mockbridge] ... to Coufold [Cowfold]'.

11 Stretham Manor. The present house was built *c*.1450, probably on the site of an earlier timber-framed house, and adjacent to the bishop's earlier moated manor house. It later became farm cottages, was restored in the early 20th century by the Jeans family, and is seen here in 1947. An extension was built onto the left-hand side in the 1970s.

The Custumal also describes the bishop's right of way over lands west of Stretham 'towards Amberle' (Amberley), where the bishop had a castle, via 'Wycham' (Wyckham), 'Hondeleston' (Huddlestone) and 'Wappyngthorne' (Wappingthorn). This makes it clear that the Roman Greensand Way was then still in use, nearly 1,000 years after the Roman legions left, although references to 'horse, gear and packhorses' indicate that it was no longer suitable for wheeled vehicles.

The Custumal lists the landholders in the manor, 88 in all, by status, and describes their holdings and their duties to their lord. Two tenants, Andrew Peuerel of le Halland (Hollands), and Richard le Graunt of Orham (Oreham) held free land by Knight service. Four tenants, Walter Catteslond (Catsland), William Ede, Walter and John Michel and Robert Wolgard held land by 'Socage' (freehold). Twenty villeins, or customary tenants, and 19 holders of 'yardlands' held sizable parcels of land, and the remaining 44 tenants held 'cots' or other small parcels of land. The Custumal provides little evidence for extensive use of open-field farming in the parish. Ferlyngs (furlongs, or blocks of arable strips) are mentioned only in a minority of the smaller holdings. The majority of the holdings were evidently self-contained farms, and many, such as Bettele (Betley), Bokewyssh (Buckwish), Catteslond (Catsland), Eastoute (Eastout), Faircock (Faircox), Holdene (Holedean), Lachmereshale (Lashmars Hall), Pokerle (Pokerlee) and Potwelle (Potwell) are instantly recognisable on the modern Ordnance Survey map.

Feudal duties varied with the holding. Some tenants such as Walter Catteslond paid rent (11s. per quarter) and was obliged to come 'to the great boonwork [at harvest time] to oversee the reapers of the Lord's corn, that they do their work well and fairly' and in return 'shall have his dinner'. More modest tenants paid a mixture of rent in money and kind, and also supplied labour. For example, Robert Hayne paid 20d. at St Thomas' Day, 20d. at Lady Day, 2d. at Midsummer, supplied three hens at Christmas, four hens and 37 eggs at Whitsun, and had to supply man and horse to harrow for two full days, to reap two acres of wheat, one acre of barley, one acre of peas or vetches and four acres of oats. He also had to provide two men at one harvest boonwork for a whole day. In addition, when the lord was in residence at Stretham, he was obliged to cart two wainloads (waggonloads) of sticks to make bowers—presumably temporary shelters to house the lord's servants. Finally, he was obliged to maintain part of the fence of Aldyngbourne Park (near Chichester, where the bishop held another manor).

The 14th century witnessed the 'Black Death', or what is usually today considered to have been bubonic plague. Outbreaks occurred over about a 30-year period, during which time an estimated 40 per cent of the population died. The Peasants' Revolt, which followed in 1381, marked the beginning of the end of the feudal system. A shortage of people to work the land gave peasants more power and enabled them to demand more rights. There is no reason to suppose that Henfield was not affected by these events. With whole families being wiped out by the plague, there was a move towards fewer and larger farms. As farmers became free of feudal ties, and able to prosper, they were able to build houses which would last. It is for this reason that many of the farmhouses scattered around the Henfield parish today were built during the late medieval and Tudor times.

12 Lashmars Hall, situated close to the river west of Henfield. It is first mentioned in the Custumal of 1374 as 'Lachmereshale' when it was held by John Nicol 'in his office of swineherd'.

13 Barrow Hill farmhouse, Shoreham Road. A good example of a Tudor farmhouse. This photograph dates from *c*.1910 when tiles hiding the timber framing were still in place. These have since been removed.

14 Chatfields, Golden Square. The original farmhouse was built *c*.1548 as a 'hall house' with open hearth in the centre. The brick chimney and an extension to the north were added about 1630. Later extensions were made in the 18th and 19th centuries.

A number of larger houses also appeared in Henfield. In addition to the old manor house at Stretham, a 'New Hall' was built on higher ground half a mile to the south-east. The manorial court is recorded as having been held there *c*.1550. Onto this was added *c*.1620, at a cost of £300, a large square house by Prosper Rainsford, a London surgeon who was a 'quarter waiter'—a courtier who attended for three months of each year—to King Charles I. The manorial court continued to be held there until the 18th century.

Henfield Place in Upper Station Road has some parts dating to 1450, and Parsonage House nearby was built by Thomas Bysshopp in Tudor times. Potwell in Cagefoot Lane was another important farmhouse built *c*.1600, whilst Backsettown in Furners Lane is a hall house, as is Bylsborough, a little further east along Furners Lane, actually in the parish of Woodmancote. To the north and west of the village are Shiprods, Eatons and

Mockbridge House. Other old farmhouses include Bottings, Buckwish, Catsfold, Rye, Dears, Lashmars Hall, Swains and Holedean.

Few new houses were built in the 18th century. The Wealden iron industry to the north was in terminal decline owing to more efficient and cheaper techniques being developed in the Midlands, and agriculture was depressed. In 1855 the population of Henfield parish was about 1,660, in 1862, one year after the railway was completed, it was virtually the same number, but by 1871 it had risen to 1,856. Development took place around the station, including *The Station Hotel*, the steam mill at the bottom of Station Road, and the gasworks in Hollands Lane. Following the arrival of the railway, as land became available, development continued to take place in the middle of the west side of the High Street. Natural boundaries of the village were set by the High Street, Church Street, Dropping Holms and Nep Town Road, and to the west by the railway and Station Road. The pace of development was slow at first, but in the mid- to late Victorian period good quality detached and terraced houses were built in Church Street, Broomfield Road, Cagefoot Lane and at Nep Town. Nep Town expanded considerably during this period, especially in the area of Weavers Lane. Development continued at a modest pace through to the start of the Great War.

The 1930s was a period for building both detached and semi-detached houses along London Road, Barrow Hill, Dropping Holms, Upper and Lower Station Roads, and along Furners Lane. The 1950s saw the construction of housing estates such as Manor Way, Manor Close, Mill Drive and Cedar Way. Increasing demand for housing in south-east England in the 1960s saw the first Henfield Village Plan being produced. Henfield had become a place for people to

15 Delightful memorial brass in the vestry of St Peter's parish church to Meneleb (d.1627), son of Prosper Rainsford of New Hall, and his grandmother Ann Kenwellmersh (d.1633), showing the elaborate dress of the day.

16 The east elevation of Henfield Place, *c.*1916. 'Horsham Stone' as a roofing material appears on a number of old properties in Henfield including Backsettown, Bylsborough, Potwell and Stretham Manor.

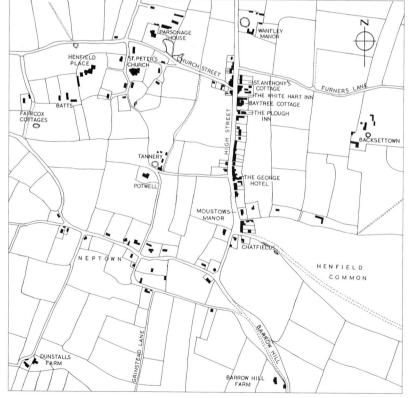

17 Map that shows Henfield, *c.*1700, with small settlements around the church and at Nep Town. The small manor of Moustows on the eastern side of the High Street sold off plots of land as small farms, whilst the western side, belonging to the Manor of Stretham, remained open land for another century.

retire to or commute from to their work on the south coast or in the towns of Horsham and Crawley to the north. Local demand for housing, coupled with a decline in the market garden industry, created a boom in housing development in the 1960s. This took place on the agricultural land through the centre of the village, to the north of Upper Station Road, and also to the east of the High Street. The development continued into the 21st century on the periphery of the village with Chess Brook Green, The Daisycroft, Chanctonbury View, and the large Parsonage Farm and Deer Park estates. The population of the village has doubled over the last 50 years, and further housing is now planned on the Deer Park estate.

18   Henfield High Street looking north, *c*.1870. Development took place in the early 1800s with the properties on the left-hand side, and had extended south to Clarence House (the present post office) by *c*.1840. The three-storey house on the left was built by Thomas Stevens, watchmaker, *c*.1860. The old timber-framed buildings on the corner of Church Street were demolished *c*.1880.

19 A good example of late Victorian building is South View Terrace in Nep Town. Built in the 1880s on the southern edge of the village, these houses can be seen from the South Downs.

20 Until *c*.1904 the only properties on the west side of the High Street between Cagefoot Lane and Golden Square were the village pound and its adjoining pound keeper's 'shanty'. The pound and 'shanty' were demolished *c*.1905, and the cottage on the left and the cottage which replaced the pound were both demolished *c*.1960.

Two

COMMUNICATIONS

AS WE HAVE SEEN, the settlements at Stretham and on the ridge occurred because of the proximity of the Roman road and the River Adur. In the following centuries, also, Henfield's periods of prosperity have been due to its presence on heavily used lines of communication. Many of the houses on the east side of the High Street were built in the late medieval period, along what had become an important road leading to Shoreham, then a major port on the south coast.

As well as the north-south road there were also roads running east-west. Furners Lane was an ancient trackway running from the High Street eastwards to the village of Blackstone, and then onwards to Albourne and Hurstpierpoint. The Ordnance Survey map shows the road running along the field boundaries, demonstrating that it is older than the fields themselves. Westward it continued in a straight line past the church and on towards the river along what is now West End Lane.

Another perhaps equally ancient trackway kept to the southern edge of the high ground and ran from Nep Town down Dropping Holms and Hollands Lane and then on to Horsebridge Common and Wiston. There was a ford of the river at New Inn, and a bridge has existed there at least since Tudor times. It gained the name Bineham Bridge in the 18th century. The bridge was washed away in 1814, when the snows of a particularly harsh winter melted, and despite public protest was not rebuilt until 1895, by which time parts of Hollands Lane had disintegrated into a footpath. The present footbridge dates from the 1950s. Even as recently as 1914 there were proposals to upgrade the trackway from Horsebridge Common to form a roadway into the village from the west.

Windmill Lane, Grinstead Lane and Dagbrook Lane were used to drive animals on and off the brooks. The section of Dagbrook Lane north of Brookside Farm probably went out of use as a trackway when the farm moved from the edge of the brooks to its present position in about the 1860s. The deep cuts at the top of Windmill Lane and Grinstead Lane testify to the amount of use which these tracks have had over the centuries.

21 *The George Hotel* is one of three coaching inns in the High Street. The oldest part, on the right, was built in *c.*1550 with a jettied upper storey to the west and north, which is still visible inside the building. This photograph shows the annual pub outing of 1912.

22 The top of Dropping Holms before the road was widened *c.*1988. The road widening paved the way for three new houses to be built along the road together with the Chanctonbury View estate, which now occupies the left of this view.

23 Looking south along Broomfield Road, *c*.1914. This was a new road built in the 1860s to serve Broomfields and properties in what is now Croft Lane, the road leading away to the right. In the late Victorian period other houses were built along the west side of the road, and in the 1960s the road was extended past Batts to join Upper Station Road.

Up until the middle of the 18th century, it had been the responsibility of parishes to maintain the roads in their district. This piecemeal administration, together with the thick clays of the Weald, led to Sussex roads being notoriously bad, and often impassable for much of the year. Some improvement came with the formation of the turnpike trusts. The road through Henfield and on to Brighton via Saddlescombe (now the A281 and Dyke Road) was 'turnpiked' in 1771. The Act of Parliament required to set up the turnpike trust also authorised the tolls to be charged: typical tolls were 6d. for a wagon drawn by two horses, 2d. for any beast not drawing a carriage, cattle 10d. per score, and sheep 5d. per score. Revenue from tolls on the Henfield to Cowfold turnpike was £345 in 1857. To travel around the local villages of Bramber, Steyning and Partridge Green using the various toll roads would have cost about 1s. 4d. Tolls were taken on the Henfield Turnpike until 1877.

All of what are now A and B roads in the area were turnpiked, with the notable exception of the road between Henfield and Upper Beeding (now A2037). This demonstrates that what had once been an important road to the coast and the port of Shoreham had now ceased to be so. The focal point for the toll roads in the central part of Sussex had become Brighton, now the most important town on the south coast. This had been a small fishing village called Brighthelmstone when first visited by George, Prince of Wales in 1783, and with his patronage had become a popular salt-water-spa resort.

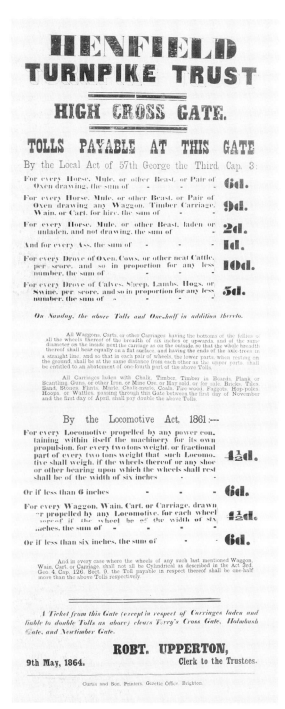

HENFIELD TURNPIKE TRUST

HIGH CROSS GATE.

TOLLS PAYABLE AT THIS GATE

By the Local Act of 57th George the Third, Cap. 3:

For every Horse, Mule, or other Beast, or Pair of Oxen drawing, the sum of	6d.
For every Horse, Mule, or other Beast, or Pair of Oxen drawing any Waggon, Timber Carriage, Wain, or Cart for hire, the sum of	9d.
For every Horse, Mule, or other Beast, laden or unladen, and not drawing, the sum of	2d.
And for every Ass, the sum of	1d.
For every Drove of Oxen, Cows, or other neat Cattle, per score, and so in proportion for any less number, the sum of	10d.
For every Drove of Calves, Sheep, Lambs, Hogs, or Swine, per score, and so in proportion for any less number, the sum of	5d.

On Sunday, the above Tolls and One-half in addition thereto.

All Waggons, Carts, or other Carriages having the bottoms of the fellies of all the wheels thereof of the breadth of six inches or upwards, and of the same diameter on the inside next the carriage as on the outside, so that the whole breadth thereof shall bear equally on a flat surface, and having the ends of the axle-trees in a straight line, and so that in each pair of wheels, the lower parts, when resting on the ground, shall be at the same distance from each other as the upper parts, shall be entitled to an abatement of one-fourth part of the above Tolls.

All Carriages laden with Chalk, Timber, Timber in Boards, Plank or Scantling, Guns, or other Iron, or Mine Ore, or Hay sold, or for sale, Bricks, Tiles, Sand, Stones, Flints, Marle, Chalk-marle, Coals, Fire wood, Faggots, Hop-poles, Hoops, or Wattles, passing through this Gate between the first day of November and the first day of April, shall pay double the above Tolls.

By the Locomotive Act, 1861 :—

For every Locomotive propelled by any power containing within itself the machinery for its own propulsion, for every two tons weight, or fractional part of every two tons weight that such Locomotive shall weigh, if the wheels thereof or any shoe or other bearing upon which the wheels shall rest shall be of the width of six inches	4½d.
Or if less than 6 inches	6d.
For every Waggon, Wain, Cart, or Carriage, drawn ⸺r propelled by any Locomotive, for each wheel ⸺rec°f if the wheel be of the width of six ⸺nches, the sum of	4½d.
Or if less than six inches, the sum of	6d.

And in every case where the wheels of any such last mentioned Waggon, Wain, Cart, or Carriage, shall not all be Cylindrical as described in the Act 3rd Geo. 4, Cap. 126, Sect. 9, the Toll payable in respect thereof shall be one-half more than the above Tolls respectively.

A Ticket from this Gate (except in respect of Carriages laden and liable to double Tolls as above) clears Terry's Cross Gate, Holmbush Gate, and Newtimber Gate.

ROBT. UPPERTON,

9th May, 1864.   Clerk to the Trustees.

Curtis and Son, Printers, Gazette Office, Brighton.

24 Tolls payable at the High Cross gate which was located about two and a half miles north-west of Henfield on the road to Twineham.

The rapid growth of Brighton between the 1780s and 1820s brought new prosperity to Henfield. Henfield lay on one of the main coaching routes between London and Brighton and the Prince Regent often passed through the village. A coach service operated daily between London and Brighton and coaches stopped at *The White Hart Inn* in the High Street for the change of horses. Another service also passed through *en route* for Oxford and Windsor, with coaches changing horses at *The George Hotel*. As well as these major routes, local carriers operated between neighbouring towns and villages. By 1825 Percy Gregory, who lived at 'Forges' at Golden Square, was operating a weekly service to Lewes, and Joseph Shoulders operated a service between Henfield and Brighton, on Thursdays, Fridays and Saturdays. The High Street was therefore a busy and important thoroughfare at this time.

Henfield became a favoured retreat for those who prospered in Brighton. The Hall and Borrer families were bankers, of the firm of Hall, West and Borrer, later the Union Bank, Eardley N. Hall becoming Treasurer of the Brighton Commissioners in 1854. Thomas Wisden, born in Henfield, whose father was a farmer and tanner, became a speculative builder and survived bankruptcy to become lord of the manor of Brighton and a major shareholder in the Chain Pier Company. The *Pigot Directory* of 1828 described Henfield thus: 'It is not a place of trade or manufacture nor does it contain anything of curiosity or interest, sufficient to stay the inquisitive traveller in his progress. Several respectable residences are in the vicinity of the village, and the country around it is replete with rural beauty.'

25 Tollgates were situated every few miles on the turnpike roads. This tollgate house was at the top of Crouch Hill at the junction of the Albourne Road, half a mile north of Henfield, and survived until the mid-1920s. Others existed at the top end of Horn Lane, Woodmancote, and at Shermanbury, where the Partridge Green road meets the A281.

26 The turnpike trust replaced Mock Bridge over the River Adur at Shermanbury in 1794. In 1930 the brick bridge shown here was replaced by the present stone structure.

27   The London to Brighton stage-coach service was revived by the American tycoon Alfred Vanderbilt between 1908 and 1914. It stopped at *The White Hart Inn* for a change of horses. Soon after the First World War a coach called 'Nimrod' made the journey, and in 1957 one called 'Red Rover'.

28   Edward Pattenden be-came one of the carriers to Brighton *c*.1850. Following his death a few years later the business was carried on by his widow Catherine and her two sons William and Walter. The photograph shows William Pattenden with the coach outside his brother Edward's grocer's shop at the top of the High Street, *c*.1895.

Many of the old medieval, Tudor and Jacobean buildings in the High Street and elsewhere were given modern façades in the period of Georgian and Regency prosperity. People were keen to portray a modern image, especially as the Prince Regent often passed by. Properties such as Moustows Manor built new rooms on the street side to hide the older building behind. Old brickwork was covered up by using stucco, as at New Hall, and timber frames were concealed with hanging tiles, such as on Mermaid Cottage opposite Furners Lane, or 'mathematical tiles' to resemble brickwork, such as the *White Hart Inn*.

The side roads such as Church Street, Furners Lane and Nep Town Road would then have been little more than dirt tracks. The occupiers of the land along them drew up agreements for their upkeep. For example, an agreement of May 1849 is for the repair of one mile, three furlongs, one rod (approx. 2,500 yds.) of West End Lane westwards from the back gate of Henfield Place. William Keywood, who lived at *New Inn* and farmed Barrows and Wicks, was responsible for the repair of 80 rods (440 yds.) of the lane; Thomas Williams, who occupied Little Lashmars (probably the present

29 New Hall, as re-modelled by banker Nathaniel Hall in the early 19th century, seen here in 1948 when it was the home of the archaeologist Sir Leonard Woolley, the discoverer of ancient Ur. He was also the mentor of T.E. Lawrence (Lawrence of Arabia) in his excavations in Palestine before the First World War. The weeping ash tree in the foreground was destroyed in the 1987 storm.

30 The original road to Blackstone, now known as Furners Lane, *c*.1912. It was also known as Sandy Lane in the early 20th century. On the right are North Cottages, Woolvens Row, and in the distance Eastern Terrace.

Subscriptions towards defraying part expense of making the Road leading from the Workhouse Barn to the Railway Station

		£	s	d
Paid E N Hall		10		
Paid Wisden Esqr		10	0	0
Revd J O Brien		1	0	0
L Borrer	Paid	5	0	0
Ch J Wisden		10		
J W Frost		5	0	0
Paid John Penikett		2	0	0
Paid Longley Brothers		10		
De Lewis		5	0	
Paid A W M Caudle		5	0	0
		48	15	0

Surveyor of the Highways

31 Subscriptions received from local dignitaries towards the upkeep of Nep Town Road, *c*.1870. At that time Eardley Hall was living in Barrow Hill House, Thomas Wisden at Moustows Manor, then called Poplar House, Lindfield Borrer at Red Oaks, then called Elm Grove, Charles Wisden in the High Street, and Henry West at Terrys Cross, Woodmancote.

Chates) and Little Betley and Great Betley, was responsible for the repair of 51 rods (280 yds.). Chalk from the pit at Saddlescombe or elsewhere on the Downs would have been used to carry out the repairs.

Although the River Adur had been used for the transport of timber in the early 18th century, it was not until the 19th century that it was made navigable for barges into its upper reaches. An Act of Parliament passed in 1807 enabled the Commissioners of Sewers for the Rape of Bramber, the body responsible for the land drainage, to collect rates from landowners above the tidal limit, improve the drainage of their land and make the river navigable from Shoreham to Bines Bridge on the west fork, and to Mock Bridge on the eastern fork. A towpath was formed for the barges and re-alignment of the river carried out, notably between Bineham Bridge and Stretham, to enable barges over 60ft. in length and drawing 4ft. of water to use the river.

Wharves were dug at Bines Bridge, Mock Bridge and along the river at places like Eatons Farm and *New Inn* to allow materials to be loaded. A second Act of Parliament in 1825 enabled the navigation to be extended on the western fork as far as Bay Bridge on the present A24 at West Grinstead. The Baybridge Canal Company constructed pound locks at Partridge Green (which still exist today) and West Grinstead, one set of 'pointing door' locks close to the fork, and another set on the east fork of the river just north of the junction. A late 19th-century Ordnance Survey map also shows a lock

32 The junction of the east and west forks of the River Adur, west of Henfield, in 2001. Locks for the Baybridge Navigation were on each fork, on the sites of the present weirs and footbridges.

33 *New Inn*, situated about a mile and a half west of Henfield close to the River Adur. Much of its trade came from bargemen and local farmers. It was bought by Charles Tobitt in 1916 and soon afterwards the licence to sell ale was surrendered.

immediately north of Bines Bridge. The authorised toll charges were 2½d./ton/mile for materials such as gravel, chalk and soil, and 5d./ton/mile for other goods. In the 1841 census, 15 men in Henfield were listed as bargemen. These came mainly from the Lelliott family who lived down West End Lane at Leeches, Bests and Knights (the last two names are not identifiable today). The coming of the railway in 1861 effectively killed off the river as a means of transport, and in the 1871 census only one bargeman is listed. The Baybridge Canal Company received so little in tolls that it was unable to pay the interest on its loan debt and was closed by Act of Parliament in 1875.

From 1835 prominent Brighton residents proposed the building of a railway to London, and six alternative schemes were proposed. By 1837 this was reduced to four, two of which, those of Stephenson and Gibbs, would have passed through Henfield. Henfield Museum has maps dating from this period which show two possible routes for the London to Brighton Railway through Henfield. They both start just to the east of Shermanbury Grange. The easterly route is shown passing through Bottings Farm at Mock Bridge, through where the Wantley estate is now, clipping the eastern corner of

Henfield Common and heading for the South Downs somewhere near Fulking. The other route is shown running almost north-south from Shermanbury Grange, passing through Cibses, south of Mock Bridge and Parsonage Farm and cutting through the village where Gresham Place and Faircox Lane are now before continuing south at the end of Sandy Lane. Another variation shows the line passing between Stretham Manor and New Hall which would have taken it through Upper Beeding rather than Bramber.

Had one of these routes been chosen, Henfield, would today resemble Burgess Hill and Wivelsfield, tiny hamlets in 1837 but now one large town. After much debate, however, the much more costly and difficult direct route was eventually chosen, and the London Brighton & South Coast Railway (L.B. & S.C.R.) main line via Haywards

34 Henfield railway station looking north, with the West End Lane bridge in the distance. Other stations on the line were at Southwater, West Grinstead, Partridge Green, Steyning and Bramber. The journey time between Henfield and Steyning was about six minutes.

35 Henfield station staff, *c.*1920. On the left are two clerks, in the centre the station master Alfred Standing, and on the right Mr Boswell the signalman and Mr Bridger the porter. In later years the station master at Steyning was also responsible for Henfield and Bramber stations.

Heath opened in 1841. Queen Victoria, who disliked Brighton, visited it for the last time in 1845, and the loss of royal patronage, together with the opening of the railway, rapidly led to the decline of the London to Brighton stagecoach through Henfield, and a lean period for the village.

In 1846 it was proposed to construct a branch line from Shoreham up to Steyning, but nothing became of this. Then, in 1857, proposals were put forward to link Shoreham with Horsham and Dorking. This became known as the 'landowners line'. The object of the scheme was to compete with the L.B. & S.C.R. for passengers travelling between London and Brighton. The proposed route kept mainly to the west of the River Adur and would have missed Henfield by about two miles. Seeing a threat to their monopoly on the London to Brighton line, the L.B. & S.C.R. came up with their own proposals for a railway down the Adur Valley.

Unlike the 'landowners line' route, this scheme aimed to link many of the villages *en route*. Both companies held public meetings to drum up support for their proposals, one such being held by the L.B. & S.C.R. at *The George Hotel* on 19 December 1857. Both schemes passed their first reading in the House of Commons and went to the committee stage in April 1858. The case for the L.B. & S.C.R. scheme was so well put by the company that it won approval. It was authorised by Act of Parliament dated 12 July 1858, at an estimated cost of £155,000, and work began in the spring of 1859. A single-track section of line between Shoreham and Partridge Green was opened on 1 July 1861, and the remainder to Itchingfield Junction on 16 September 1861. The whole length had double track by 1879.

A century later, a major local event of the 1960s was the closure of the railway under the 'Beeching Plan'. In May 1963 the parish council decided to protest to West Sussex County Council and Chanctonbury Rural District Council about the proposed closure, on the grounds that a bus service would not be able to handle all the types of goods carried by the railway. Questionnaires were distributed to the railway users and in early 1964 a public inquiry was held at Steyning to consider the hardship which would be caused if the line were to close. The only chance of saving the railway from closure would have been to prove that the bus service would be inadequate. The evidence was heard at the South East Region Traffic Commissioner's Court held in Brighton in November 1965, and a decision came in December 1965 to proceed to issue licences for additional bus services. This sealed the fate of the railway, and the line closed in March 1966. The concrete steps which led down to the station entrance still exist at the northern end of the Beechings estate.

Although the loss of the railway was mourned by railway enthusiasts and sentimental residents alike, there can be no doubt that Henfield would be a very different place today had it remained. Comparable villages which are still served by railways, such as Pulborough and Billingshurst, have expanded greatly, whilst Henfield's post-war expansion has been relatively modest. It is sobering to consider that the large town of Haywards Heath did not exist at all before the opening of the London to Brighton

36 Henfield's telephone operators in Croft House, High Street in the 1960s. From left to right: Mrs P. Meredith, Mrs Basil Nicholls, Trixie Hellier, Mrs Short, Mrs John Nicholls and Dorothy Middleton (supervisor).

railway in 1841, and that the railway company were at a loss to know what to name their new station.

The telephone came to Henfield *c.*1902, and the first exchange was run by Mr Downer from a house in Park Road. In later years it moved to an upstairs room in Croft House in the High Street, where it remained until an automatic exchange was built in the 1960s. The first public telephone in the village was inside William Powell's shop which was situated in the High Street opposite Clarence House.

Three

HENFIELD AT WORK

IT IS PERHAPS DIFFICULT TODAY to appreciate the amount of industry which was formerly present in Henfield. From the 1828 *Pigots Directory* of shopkeepers and traders we can see that Henfield had two tailors, four carpenters, two butchers, four boot and shoe makers, two grocers, two drapers, two saddlers, one clockmaker, three millers, one wheelwright, four blacksmiths, one painter and glazier, and one tanner. The geology of the area greatly influenced its former principal industries, namely brickmaking, tanning, farming and market gardening. The Weald Clay to the north and south of the village has been used for brickmaking for centuries, many of the older houses being built from locally made bricks. Early brickmakers would have simply dug a hole in the Weald Clay near the site of a proposed house. A wooden mould was used to form the bricks, which were then left to dry in the sun. The bricks were fired in a clamp, a stack of the dried bricks intermingled with suitably placed charcoal, the whole then covered in turf, and the fire lit. The clamp would burn for several weeks, and needed careful attention to ensure that the correct temperatures were attained.

The sites of some of these early brickyards can be identified in field names. To the north of 'The Pools', just off the A2037, there is a field called 'brickfield', and next to it another called 'limekiln field'. To the west, a field close to Lipride is similarly called 'brick kiln field'. There must have been many more brickmaking sites of which no trace remains today. The first commercial brickyard was probably on the western end of Broadmere Common. It was in existence by 1735, and is still shown on the 1875 Ordnance Survey map. This brickworks seems to have been operated by Richard Bound who died in 1749, and later by his son Thomas until his death in 1773. R. Pattenden Snr advertised for a tenant for the house and brick kilns in 1816. Some of the ponds on the common are old clay pits, commons being used for brickyards because they were often poor land with a thin soil and clay close to the surface; there was also brushwood available for firing bricks. George Morley was a brickmaker on Broadmere Common between 1867 and 1874. The tenant of a brickfield south of Eastout on the 1844 tithe map was James Hoadley.

37 Cottage on Broadmere Common. What is now 'The Pond House' used to be called 'Kiln Cottage'. The brickyard behind the property was closed by manorial authority in 1878, at the time when the manor of Stretham was being broken up and sold.

In 1934 another brickworks was started by Southwick builder R.H. Penny on the Shoreham road at the site of the present 'Builder Centre' yard. The business was sold to Ambrose Congreve in 1952. In 1965, when production was at its height, it employed 44 people and produced 200,000 Sussex stock bricks a week. These were a particularly hard brick used all over Sussex and for tall flats in London. The brickworks had been in financial difficulty for a number of years, and when it was put up for sale in 1969 it failed to find a buyer and closed, putting 31 men out of work.

Running east-west through the centre of the village are the Folkestone beds, consisting of a loose yellow sand. When houses were built on this ground, small pits would be dug to obtain sand for their construction. This happened at Southview Terrace, and probably also at Commercial Buildings in the High Street. Large sandpits on the south-facing slopes of the Henfield ridge were started in the late 19th century. That at Sandy Lane was dug by hand and worked out by the 1930s. This sandpit was originally owned by Philip Hedgecock and later taken over by Brighton Corporation, possibly on his death in 1903. After the Second World War there were allotments at the southern end of the pit and chickens were kept in the northern part.

On the east side of Windmill Lane a new pit dug by machine in 1935 was fully excavated by the beginning of the war. Afterwards the Greenfield family had a market

38 Henfield Brickworks in 1965. Bricks were moved in and out of the Hoffman-type continuous kiln using these hand barrows.

39 Workmen with their families in the Sandy Lane sandpit around the time of the First World War. On the ladder is Bill Carter, and next to him Ethel and Nellie Carter. Sand was shovelled into trucks which were pushed on a tramway down to the railway where they were tipped up and the sand discharged into railway wagons waiting in the siding.

garden in the northern part of the pit, paying £31 10s. a year rent, and David Stephens had a sawmill on the southern half. He used to sell logs, and in 1948 was paying 13s. 6d. per month rent. The sand pit at the back of Henfield Common was dug c.1874 and it is believed that much of the sand was used for building St Hugh's Charterhouse monastery at Cowfold.

Sandstone from the Hythe beds is exposed on three sides of the Henfield ridge. Strangely, it has only been excavated at one place, in what is now known as Stonepit Lane. The rock is an excellent building stone, and was used in the 14th century for rebuilding St Peter's Church. The stone was dug as and when required, but has only survived in about half a dozen houses in the village.

One of the most important industries in the village was tanning. There were tanyards at Steyning and Horsham, but that at Henfield was the most important in this part of Sussex in the 16th and 17th centuries. Cattle kept on the brooks provided hides for boots, shoes, harness, saddles and leather buckets. Pig, sheep, and goat skins provided thin leather for gloves, bags and jackets, and vellum for legal documents. The tanning process was slow, messy and foul smelling, and needed a great deal of water. The Henfield Tanyard had two natural ponds fed by springs. The other requirements for tanning were also readily available: lime produced by burning chalk from the Downs; and tannic acid from oak bark from the many woods in the area. The highly polluted effluent from the tanyard ran through open ditches and under Church Street onto Parsonage Farm, and the little green in Church Street was aptly named Pinchnose Green.

Tanning probably began in Henfield in the medieval period, and in the mid-16th century there were reputed to have been four tanners living in the village. In the early 17th century William Rootes and Edward Geoff were tanners, as were the Haynes family in the 18th century. *The White Hart Inn* was known at one time as 'the special house of the tanners'. Many craftsmen associated with tanning were also to be found in the village. There were saddle and harness makers, glove and gaiter makers, and in the 1830s the village boasted five boot and shoe makers. The tanyard closed in 1844, the last tanner being William Wisden. The field remained as pasture until 1986 when proposals were made to develop it for housing. This aroused much local opposition, but in the end a compromise was reached, and only one acre was developed, in exchange for the remaining three acres, including the pond, becoming a permanent open space. A 19th-century building associated with the tanning business has also survived.

The pattern of farms in the district was laid down in Saxon times, and apart from those close to the village which were built over in the 20th century, such as Staples Barn Farm, Wantley Farm and Parsonage Farm, has remained largely unchanged. In the 17th century the houses on the east side of the High Street were farmhouses with their land going eastwards. As the land was always leased from the Bishops of Chichester, the farms remained small. New Hall or Stretham Farm, the 'home farm' of the bishops, has always been the largest in the parish, at about 400 acres.

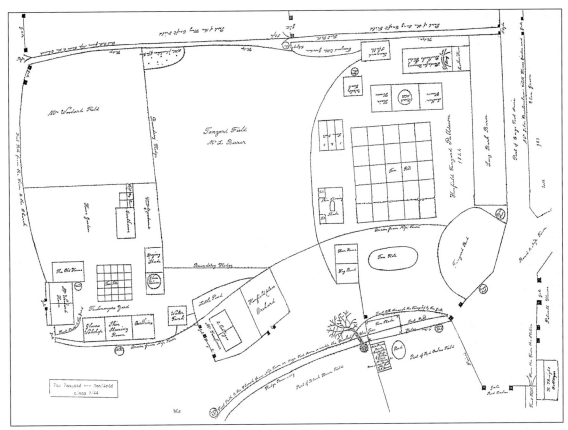

40 Map of Tanyard in 1844, drawn from memory *c.*1860. There were actually two tanyards in Henfield. That by the pond in Cagefoot Lane dealt with cattle hides, and the other, further north behind Tannery Cottage in Church Street, tanned pig, sheep and goat skins.

The Yeakell and Gardner map produced in the late 18th century shows all the brookland devoted to pasture, but more arable land down West End Lane and between the brooks and the Shoreham Road than there is today. Woodland totalled about 50 acres, the largest areas being Hoe Wood near Woodsmill, outside the parish boundary, and the remains of Parsonage Wood bordering on the Chess Brook.

The brooks along the River Adur provided hay and rich summer pasture for the cattle. The bishops relied on this for their supply of beef and, according to the 1374 custumal, it was the task of one of the tenants to walk the cattle from Stretham to his landlord's castle at Amberley, a distance of 20 miles. Dairy farming was common until the middle of the 20th century, and local farms would supply all of Henfield with milk and dairy products. Farms on the clay lands have traditionally been mainly arable, growing wheat, barley and, in the past, root crops for fodder. More recently, oilseed rape, forage maize and linseed have been grown.

41 Brookside Dairy, which was established by the Harmes family in 1906, is seen here making deliveries in Weavers Lane, Nep Town in the early 1920s. Barrow Hill Farm, Catsfold Farm, and Mr A. Heasman at Potwell all made local milk deliveries before the Second World War as well.

Revolutionary improvements in agriculture in the 18th and 19th centuries did little, however, to improve the living conditions of agricultural labourers, who in 1841 made up about 40 per cent of the working population. Many lived below subsistence level and received parish relief. Under the Poor Laws, each parish was responsible for looking after its own 'destitutes', and to do this rates were levied. The scheme was administered by the churchwardens and 'overseers of the poor'. In 1827, when the population of Henfield was about 1,000, almost 10 per cent were receiving parish relief. Eleven widows received monthly sums of between 5s. and £2, 16 sick and infirm people received between 5s. and £1 4s., four illegitimate children received between 10s. and 12s. and a large group of 65 people classed as 'others' received between 5s. and £2. The total burden on the rates for December 1827 amounted to £118 5s. 9d.

Agricultural labourers were also often recruited as casual labour for smuggling gangs, and this provided an extra source of income. Smuggling was at its height in Sussex during the 18th century because of the crippling Customs and Excise Duty levied on many luxury goods such as tea, brandy, fine wines, silks and lace. Wool was smuggled out on the return trips to France and the Low Countries. Shoreham was the nearest Channel port to London, and the Adur valley provided a convenient route northwards for smuggled goods. Contraband was sometimes landed at Bineham Bridge, and there are stories of secret tunnels at *New Inn*, smuggled goods being hidden in the sand caves at Hundred Steddle and in table graves in Henfield churchyard. In December 1778 a convoy of two hundred armed smugglers was recorded as having openly passed through the High Street with seven captured 'preventive men'. More commonly, smuggled goods passed quietly north along the track to the east of Henfield Common, avoiding the High Street.

With the expansion of Brighton in the 19th century, the market gardens around it on the fertile coastal soil, which had fed the growing population, were soon built over. The rich sandy soil running through the centre of Henfield became market gardens to replace them. All available land on the ridge and its southern slopes was intensively cultivated, and a variety of crops was grown. Many of the families living in Nep Town were employed on the market gardens. In the last quarter of the 19th century a nursery with glasshouses was built at Springlands at the southern end of Windmill Lane. From the early 1900s onwards nurseries began to appear behind Kindersley, in Upper Station Road, and along West End Lane. A peak was reached in the 1960s when there were about nine in operation. These tended to specialise in cut flowers, tomatoes, soft fruit, salad crops and mushrooms. Until the age of motor vehicles, produce was taken to Brighton Market by horse and cart about three times a week. An extra pair of horses was

42 The Henfield workhouse, on the edge of the Rothery Field in Nep Town Road, was built in 1736 and remained in use until 1834 when the Poor Law Amendment Act created large workhouses for groups of parishes or 'unions'. The Henfield poor were sent to the Steyning Union Workhouse at Shoreham, which later became Southlands Hospital. Today the Henfield workhouse is three cottages.

usually needed to pull the heavy loads up Dale Hill at Pyecombe. Having completed that task, the pair would then be brought back to Henfield. The coming of the railway in 1861 opened up the London markets such as Covent Garden, and specialist crops and cut flowers were usually sent there.

The market gardens and nurseries remained prosperous until the late 1960s, when they declined due to competition from larger growers along the coast. A few more nurseries have opened since, but only a few of those which existed in the 1960s remain today. Swains Farm, run by the Hills family, and earlier the Standen family, on the edge of Henfield Common is still a thriving market garden business. Over the years the Hills have taken on more land and opened a farm shop. Another market garden family still in business is the Whites of Holdean Farm, who have been in Henfield for more than 150 years. Many more families have been associated with market gardening in the past, including five generations of the Greenfield family, who cultivated the southern part of Henfield for more than a century, including the land on which the village hall now stands. Several members of the Parsons, Heavers, Standen and Browning families were also market gardeners at one time.

Furners Farm was purchased by Eric Whittome in 1922 and planted with apple trees in 1924, becoming Gills Orchard. Some 43 varieties of apples were grown, some experimentally, along with plums, soft fruit, broad beans, sweet corn and vegetables. When Eric Whittome retired in 1970, his son Donald took over control, and a pick-your-own enterprise was introduced. This was very popular with the villagers until the farm closed in 1995 on Donald Whittome's retirement.

43 General view of market gardens on the south side of the village in the 1920s. This land below South View Terrace was cultivated by the Greenfield family for many years.

44   Boxing Day shoot, *c.*1913. The photograph was taken on the market garden behind *The George Hotel* and shows Jim Greenfield (fifth man from right) with his children Frank, Alice and Bill. On the extreme left is George Shepherd and next to him Ernest Honey. The two men in the centre with guns are Mr Walls and Mr Welling.

45   Tom Browning with cup for the best kept market garden under 50 acres in 1947. The Browning family held this market garden below the Rothery Field before moving to Woodmancote. Also in the photograph from left to right are: Mrs Harry Dale, Harry Dale, Alf Dale. The horses were kept in the barn on the corner of Nep Town Road (now converted into a house).

46 Tending the violets at the Violet Nurseries in 1912. Each morning, for seven months of the year, 5,000 freshly picked violets would be skilfully packed, taken to Henfield Station by pony and trap, and dispatched all over the country. In the background are the glass bells which covered individual plants.

47 Attractive gifts would be hand-made in the workroom in Lavender Cottage. Miss D. Bateman is seen here sewing violet sachets, *c*.1921.

In 1905 a Miss Allen and a Miss Brown started a violet nursery at Lavender Cottage on the western end of Henfield Common. Violets were the main crop, but carnations, sweet peas and lavender were also grown. The two ladies lived at Holmgarth (now called Providence Cottage), and Lavender Cottage alongside was used as a workroom. The ladies traded under the name 'Misses A & D Allen-Brown', and rose at 5 a.m. in the summer and 7 a.m. in the winter to tend the plants. The violet varieties grown were 'Princess of Wales' and 'La France'. Plants grown in the field would each be covered by a bell-shaped glass, there being 750 in all. The best violets were, however, grown in glasshouses, and won medals at Royal Horticultural Society Shows in 1921, 1922 and 1923.

Women from the village were employed to work in the violet fields and workroom, where a wide range of scented toiletries and other products were prepared. A small number of men were employed to do the heavy work of digging and watering. The business soon outgrew the original acre around the cottage, and by 1929 an additional three and a half acres of land around the village were being cultivated. The violet nurseries attracted many visitors, and had exalted patrons including Queen Alexandra and a number of duchesses. It became a popular day's outing to go over the nursery, buy violets and gifts, and then have a picnic on Henfield Common.

The nursery was sold to Allwood Brothers Ltd of Wivelsfield in 1947 to act as a stock nursery, supplying seeds and cuttings of their special varieties of carnations, pinks and dianthus. The A & D Allen-Brown business continued to produce violet-scented toilet preparations in Lavender Cottage until the last of the partners, Miss Allen died in 1952. The business was taken over by the local chemist, where the preparations were sold until the 1960s.

A study of the Henfield census returns for 1841 shows that about 15 per cent of the working population were in domestic service. The large houses such as Chestham Park and Barrow Hill had many servants, but much smaller properties would employ one or two. When the tithe map of Henfield was produced in the 1840s, the Hall and Borrer families of New Hall and Barrow Hill were the largest landowners in the parish, owning nearly 20 per cent of the land. Next came Lucretia Wood of Chestham Park, the widow of John Wood, with about 15 per cent which included most of the land on the west side of the High Street. Then came the Rt. Hon. Robert Curzon of Parham, near Storrington, and Thomas Wisden of Martyn Lodge, with about 10 per cent each. Four families therefore owned more than half of the land in the parish subject to tithes, approximately 2,000 acres in all.

In 1086, at the time of Domesday Book, there were two watermills in the vicinity of Henfield, one of which was in the Manor of Stretham on the Woods Mill stream one and a half miles to the south. The location of this mill cannot be determined accurately, but was probably at or near the present Woods Mill. The Woods Mill stream rises from springs at the foot of the South Downs at Poynings and Edburton and has supported at least two other watermills along its length.

48 Chestham Park, north of Henfield, the home of John and Lucretia Wood, was built between 1816 and 1830. It was noted for its large oak trees in the surrounding parkland, one of which measured 25ft. in circumference.

49 Domestic staff at Henfield Lodge, Woodman-cote, *c.*1919. Back row, from left to right: Bert Prince, Edie Holder (housemaid), Ada Hammond (parlour maid), Reg Knapp (chauffeur). Middle row: Maggie Malthouse (kitchen maid), Mrs Brooker (cook/house-keeper), unknown (house-maid). Front row: unknown, Florrie Roberts (lady's maid).

Woods Mill was an active cornmill until 1927. The 19th-century records show that millers tended to run in families, and some worked a number of mills in the area. From 1819-57 the millers at Woods Mill were the Botting family. From 1857-81 George Holman was miller, followed by David Burgess Atkins in 1882, and finally from 1883-1927 the Coote family, Caleb Coote being the last miller. For a while in the 1930s the mill became a tea garden. It then changed hands several times until Dr Douglas Smith purchased the millhouse and meadows in 1950. He allowed the Sussex Trust for Nature Conservation (now the Sussex Wildlife Trust) to use the site from 1966, and in 1968 bequeathed it to them.

A short distance downstream was West Mill, which could have been *Westmule* mentioned in 1226, and again in 1553 when it is called 'New Mill' and worked in conjunction with Woods Mill. During the 19th century it became well known as an oilseed mill, and in 1847 the demand for oilcake kept the mill in full employment day and night. It reverted back to corn in 1850 but had ceased working by 1882. No trace remains today of the mill which was located close to the modern house called West Mill Farm.

The other mill mentioned in Domesday Book was in the Manor of Wantley. Its site was north of Furners Lane and may have been on a stream feeding the Chess Brook rather than on the brook itself. By 1374 another watermill had appeared, probably at Buckwish, just to the west of the village. There is a wet depression on the west side of the track leading to Rye Farm which could have been the site of the millpond fed from springs at Dropping Holms. By 1575 it appears that either the Wantley or Buckwish mill had become disused.

50 Woods Mill, *c.*1912, when Charles Coote was the miller. The mill must have been rebuilt many times since the 11th century. The present structure dates from 1712 and is four storeys high. The last modification was a new pen trough in 1854. The mill has been restored to working order in recent years by the Sussex Wildlife Trust.

There are windmills recorded in Sussex in 1155, but the earliest record of one in Henfield is *c*.1575. This may have been the mill which in 1612 stood near Canons in Hollands Lane. The most likely site was the field on the south-eastern corner of the crossroads formed by Hollands Lane and Buckwish Lane, which is still called Millfield. The mill mentioned at the time of the survey of the Manor of Stretham in 1647 may be this mill, but it is more likely to have been that at Nep Town. In the court rolls of 1713 a Mrs Sheppherd was paying rent on the windmill, house and lands. The mention of a millhouse points to Nep Town where the old millhouse still survives, and a map dating from 1724 confirms the existence of a windmill on this site. Three members of the Vinall family were millers there in the 18th century. Jonathan Botting was miller from 1838-58, George Holman from *c*.1866-70, and the last miller was Clement Knight from 1874-8.

51 *Above left.* Photograph of the Nep Town windmill taken by Dr F. Lewis in 1885. The mill was situated on high ground 70 yards west of Windmill Lane and was blown down in a gale in 1908. Nep Town appears in a number of forms: Neptowne, Kneptowne, and Uptowne. 'Knep' is old English for top or high, which suitably describes its location.

52 *Left.* The windmill on the Lydds, *c*.1910, known as the New Mill, or Barringer's Mill. This was situated 50 yards east of the millhouse which was built *c*.1880. In *c*.1870 a steam mill was installed in the building on the north side of the millhouse. On the top of the mill can be seen the observatory built for John Eardley Hall.

Another windmill was built *c*.1820 to the south of Henfield Common overlooking the steep south-facing slopes known as the Lydds. This mill was larger than that at Nep Town, being about 40ft. high and on three floors. It was still working in 1898 and probably ceased about 1900 when it became much cheaper to grind corn elsewhere. An extra floor was added at the top of the mill whilst it was still working and used as an observatory by John Eardley Hall of Barrow Hill House. During the Second World War the mill was used as a lookout point by the Home Guard, and it was demolished in 1953. The millers have been recorded as Robert Stevens from 1828-60, Henry Barringer from 1866-78, and Charles Packham from 1887. It was known as the New Mill or Barringer's Mill. Another windmill which existed locally was in the Manor of Ewhurst, near Shiprods, a house one and three quarter miles north of Henfield. The site is marked by a wood called Windmill Shaw. This mill probably only existed for a short period around the middle of the 19th century when the farmer at Shiprods was listed as a miller in the trade directories.

With a plentiful supply of coal brought by the railway, a steam cornmill was built close to the station *c*.1872. The large brick building still survives today, having gone out of use after a short life *c*.1900; it could not compete with much larger mills such as Prewitt's of Horsham, or Tidey's of Partridge Green. The building has had a variety of uses since it ceased grinding corn. It was at various times a coachworks, a factory for water purifiers, and a medicine pill factory during the Second World War. After the war it was a depot for S.C.A.T.S. supplying agricultural feeds, and from 1962-92 it was used as a furniture depository for Wardens of Henfield, removers and carriers. It is now used by building contractors.

The wind, water and steam mills in the area gave rise to a need for millwrights. Some time before 1839 James Neale had founded a business as iron and brass founder and millwright in Nep Town. In the 1851 census Neale was described as millwright and master engineer, employing two men. The inscription 'J. Neale, Millwright 1844' was found on a casting on the windmill which stood south of Henfield Common. By 1854 he had been joined by William Cooper, and the business transferred to a site in the High Street. This is confirmed by the pen trough of Woods Mill, which is marked 'Neale & Cooper Millwrights 1854'. By 1862 William Cooper was running the business alone, occupying premises between the Congregational church and Norton House. Cooper's name can be found on castings in six watermills in the area, and he is known to have worked on at least six other mills in Sussex.

When William Cooper died in 1876 the business was carried on by his wife Harriet. The company diversified into hiring out agricultural machinery such as steam ploughs, threshing machines and seed cleaning machines. The business and workforce of 22 people were later managed by Robert Fowler, and in 1885 he took over the firm from Mrs Cooper. In 1895 the business was moved to Golden Square, where it continued to operate until about 1906. Coopers Yard was sold to Mr Tobitt the grocer in 1904, and he used the premises as a furniture store and place to keep his delivery carts. Around

53 Cooper's Yard in the High Street before demolition in 1967. The site, which measured only 83ft. by 110ft., contained 11 buildings. There was the two-storey carpenter's shop with lean-to office, seen here on the left, a wheelwright's shop, blacksmith's shop with two forges, cart lodge, stable and various storage buildings.

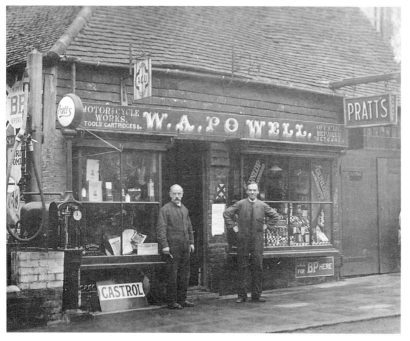

54 Mr Powell on the left outside his shop in the High Street. The photograph also shows the first petrol pump in the village. Mr Powell came to Henfield in 1900 as a cycle maker but by *c.*1913 was calling himself a motor engineer. He was in fact the first in the village to own a motor car. He retired in 1936, selling the business to F.F. Aley Ltd.

the time of the Second World War it was also used by F.F. Aley Ltd, motor engineers, as a place to work on vehicles. In the 1960s the site was acquired by British Telecom, who provided access across it to the new telephone exchange. Later the buildings on the site were demolished, and in 1977 Coopers Way was built to provide access to the new Village Hall. Efforts were made in the early 1980s to try to keep the remainder as a public open space. Pledges totalling £14,850 were made to buy the site from the owners, but they would not accept offers of less than £60,000 as outline planning permission had been granted for two shops with offices above. This last remaining part of what had been the millwright's premises was finally developed in 1989.

Blacksmiths have always been among the most important men in the village. Many people relied on their skills, not only for shoeing horses, but to make tools and iron-mongery such as hinges, which can be bought off the shelf today but which then had all to be made by hand. The skills of blacksmiths were handed down from father to son,

55 The present forge halfway along the High Street, *c*.1917. On the left, holding the horse, is George Holkham and on the right are J. White, M. Brown and A. Brown. The short man in the centre is John Brazier.

and generations of the same families have served the village. In 1636 blacksmith John Mercer, of the High Street, married Mary Woolgar and received, as her marriage settlement, a plot of land and 'tenement' adjoining the High Street between the present *Plough Inn* and the Congregational church. This remained a blacksmith's until purchased by William Powell in 1900. The ancient cottages which formed the premises were demolished and three shops built on the site *c.*1971.

In the 18th century there were three blacksmith's shops in the High Street. That which stood on the site of Prospect Cottage in Golden Square was demolished when the house was built in 1731. At least three generations of the Hider family worked the High Street forges, occupying them both from 1828-90. John Brazier came to Henfield in 1900 to take over the 17th-century forge close to *The George Hotel*. He was assisted by other blacksmiths including J. White and George Holkham, and *c.*1923 he was joined by Tom Miles, at a time when there were still some 165 working horses in the village. Miles soon took over the business from Mr Brazier, was joined by his son Harold, and in 1948 together they purchased the premises. The business is now run by Tom's grandson Alan, but the old building has become too small for the type of work being carried out, and it will shortly move elsewhere. A forge at Nep Town was long associated with the Holkham family. This began with Richard Holkham from the 1830s and his family continued to occupy the forge until the 1890s. Alfred Jennings, who died in 1943 and was renowned for his tuned shepherds' crooks, was the last blacksmith at Nep Town.

By the 1920s the age of the motor car had arrived, and two other garages opened in the High Street. John Albert Brazier, son of the blacksmith, opened his garage at

56 Tom Miles working in the High Street forge, 1966.

57 Brazier's garage in the 1920s, built by John Roberts of Cowfold. John Albert Brazier is standing on the right and just in view on the far right is the petrol pump.

Golden Square in 1923 on the site of an old cottage named 'Hewitts'. A little further along the street, opposite Rus House, Alex and John Betchley opened their garage in the early 1930s having previously occupied the old steam mill.

Another craftsman essential to a village was a wheelwright. The name of John Martin, wheelwright and carpenter, appears in *Kelly's Directory* from 1828-87, and he was followed by his son James, wheelwright and builder through to *c.*1895. The family worked from the premises in Golden Square which many people later remember as Baigent's the builders. In a building on the opposite side of the road George Lidbetter was making wheels from 1838-72.

The old timber-framed houses of the village were built by skilled craftsmen, but we have little idea of their names. More recently, *Pigot's Directory* for 1832 lists George Vinall and George Ward, bricklayers, and Arthur Brook, William Martin and John Ward, carpenters. It was not until the late 19th century that the Martin and Vinall families were described as builders. In 1899 John Terry Bishop came to Henfield and set up his building business in Cooper's Yard, and in 1907 he moved to Golden Square where he was joined in 1911 by Alfred Baigent. This partnership continued until 1917, by which time Baigent was in sole control of the firm. On the retirement of Baigent in 1957, Arthur Hobbs and Alfred Farrell, both long established employees, went into partnership and ran the firm until 1970. Their premises next to the fire station had a well-equipped workshop with machinery driven by a 1910 26 h.p. gas engine which had been

58 A view from Martins' wheelwright's yard looking north along the High Street, *c*.1890. In the foreground on the right is Ganders Cottage, and in the centre distance the forge and Rus House. On the left is *The George* field and in the distance what is now the Henfield Club on the corner of Cagefoot Lane.

59 It was the blacksmith who finally finished a wheel by putting the steel tyre on it. This is being carried out, *c*.1910, by Mr Brazier on the verge opposite the forge where the steel plate on which the wheel sat can still be seen today in front of the car wash of the nearby garage.

installed in 1925. In later years electric motors were fitted to the various machines. Over the years, the firm built council houses in Hollands Road and on the west side of New Wantley, sheltered accommodation in Fabians Way, Martyn Close, and a large number of other semi- and detached houses around the village.

The other main building firm in the village has long been Vinalls, in Nep Town Road, although the family connection disappeared in 1947 when Richard Vinall sold the business to B.S. Wilson and Alf Gander. Vinalls built the second half of New Wantley in the 1940s and went on to build a number of estates in Henfield including Manor Way and Manor Close, Furners Mead, Hewitts, Flower Farm Close and the Daisycroft. When Vinalls took over Baigents in 1970, the total workforce was 105 people. When large new estates such as Parsonage Farm on the outskirts of the village were built, the work was carried out by large national building and civil engineering firms, not by small local builders. Vinalls went into receivership in the mid-1990s, but the firm continues to trade on a smaller scale.

60 Mr Baigent wearing a bowler hat outside his workshop, *c*.1920. Upstairs are Edward Sayers and Spelzar Chowne. On the left are Ron Sayers and Wilfred Chowne, and holding the horse Bill Browning. The 19th-century building is now offices.

61 A group of bricklayers and carpenters, probably working for the Vinalls, with the tools of their trades, *c*.1900.

62 The largest brewery in the area was at Mockbridge House. The Hughes family were maltsters and coal merchants there from 1828-58. They were followed by members of the Bowler family until *c.*1915. Coal and raw materials for brewing were brought up river to Mock Bridge by barge. Here we see the delivery wagon of Frank Bowler, the last brewer, doing its rounds.

63 Cottages at Broadmere Common, where basket-making took place. The little two-storey building seen on the right, and the other at the far end of the cottages, were the withy shops. The willows would be cut, stripped of their bark, and then stored upstairs, and the baskets would be made on the ground floor.

The village used to have a number of small brewers. The Beehive Brewery was located on the site of the garage at Golden Square. From *c*.1838-50, Edward Bignell and his daughter Maria had an off-licence in what is now the *Golden Hen*, and next door at Forges Nathan Harwood was a small brewer in 1840. In Nep Town Road, for a short time around 1870, James Rich had a brewery behind Rosemount on the corner of Windmill Lane. Malthouse Cottage at the back of Henfield Common indicates the site of another brewery. On the site of the present *Henfield Tavern* in the High Street stood an old timber-framed house which became *The Old Bell*. William Parsons was a brewer here from 1856-66 and had an off-licence.

The *Kelly's Post Office Directories* of 1838-1938 list a number of other small village industries. Peter Ward, a gun and cartridge maker, started his business in Henfield in 1825. The family business carried on for another 80 years based at 5 London Road. In 1838 William Stringer was listed as a straw bonnet maker, as was Mrs Spilsbury for about 30 years from 1845. In later years another straw bonnet maker, Sarah Tugwell (later Greenfield), worked from St Anthony's Cottage in the High Street. As well as being a gaiter maker, William Morley also made cricket bats. A number of women were dress

64 Gas was used to provide street lighting around the village and domestic lighting in the larger houses. The gas lamp shown here was at the junction of Blackgate Lane and Nep Town Road. On the left is Mr Wright standing in the door of his grocer's shop. This remained a shop until 1988.

65 Gas Works Cottages in Hollands Lane with council houses in the distance, *c*.1930. These cottages were declared unfit for habitation in 1937 and were demolished in the 1960s, a dairy being built on the site.

makers, working mainly from home. There were four basket makers in the late 19th century, including William Woolgar and Alfred Brooker of Broadmere Common; it is said that William Borrer planted the willow trees or withies around the two ponds just to the west of Holdean Farm to provide them with raw materials. On the east side of the road opposite Broadmere Common there is a row of three cottages: the southernmost is Broadmere Farmhouse, but the other two were once known as Basket Makers Cottages.

Watch and clock makers have a long association with the village, perhaps beginning with James Bailey, at Clock House in the High Street in the early 19th century. London House next to *The Henfield Tavern* was built by Thomas Stevens, clock and watch maker in the 1850s, and it continued in this use until 1987. A wall clock made by Thomas Stevens is still in the church tower. In the museum and parish council office are examples of clocks made by members of the Cramp family, who were at London House from 1882-1909.

The Henfield Gas and Coke Company was formed in 1864 and sited adjacent to the railway line in Hollands Lane. Two Henfield residents, Charles Wisden and John Fairs Martin, were the original directors. The site had two gas holders, a retort house and a plant for removing harmful substances such as ammonia from the gas. From the company's report for 1887, the sale of gas and rentals amounted to £379 7s. 10d., and by-products of the process, coke, tar and breeze, sold for for £52 2s. 8d. The company had £2,502 in its capital account. A lamp lighter was employed by the parish council to turn the lights on and off. In 1911 he was paid 7s. per week, and an extra 1s. 6d. for cleaning the gas lamps. The last entry in lamplighter Bill Burt's wage book was: 'April 1st 1932—taking down lamp—7s. 6d.' By the 1950s, gas was no longer produced at Henfield but piped from Hassocks. The site was demolished in the late 1960s.

Four

THE HEART OF HENFIELD

HENFIELD'S PARISH CHURCH, dedicated to St Peter, is built on one of the highest parts of the Henfield ridge, probably on the site of the original wooden Saxon church of 770. A new church of Caen stone, brought from France up the River Adur, was erected around 1250. This would have consisted only of the chancel and nave, and all that remains of this church today is the chancel arch, two narrow lancet windows now in the clergy vestry, and part of the piscina. In the 14th century the church was enlarged by moving the north wall outwards, and replacing it with large sturdy columns and arches. The roof was raised and the south porch also added around this time. In the 15th century the buttressed tower was added and a chapel built to the north of the chancel, probably as a Lady Chapel. Now known as the Parham Chapel, this commemorates the Bysshopp family of Parsonage House and Parham House near Storrington.

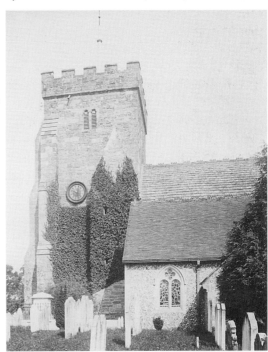

William Borrer added galleries on the north and south sides to enlarge the church in 1833, then, in 1871, drastic changes were made. The medieval roof timbers were exposed, the galleries removed, and north and south aisles and transepts were built, producing the church we see today. In March 1967 the Victorian Parish Rooms opposite the church were demolished and the new St Peter's Church House was built on the site. The money for the building came mainly

66 The southern elevation of St Peter's Church, *c.*1895. The clock seen here was replaced by one with chimes, paid for by public subscription to commemorate Queen Victoria's Diamond Jubilee in 1897.

from the sale of the Eardley Hall Institute in the High Street. Celebrations for 1,200 years of St Peter's Church took place over a week in June 1970, which included a children's pageant, flower festival and sports including mixed stoolball, ladies' football and a barbecue. In 1999 urgent repairs were again needed to the roof, and the floor has to be replaced. In 2001 plans were drawn up to allow the interior to be adapted to meet the changing needs of the congregation and to enable greater use of this magnificent building.

St Peter's has fine stained glass windows dating from the 19th and 20th centuries, some by C.E. Kempe and Geoffrey Webb. A brass to Thomas Bysshopp of 1559 is by the altar in the Parham Chapel, below a memorial tablet to his grandson Henry Bysshopp. In the church are 300 kneelers depicting the flora and fauna of the village made by the St Peter's Guild of Tapisseurs between 1983 and 1988. The tower contains a ring of eight bells, mostly dating from the 18th century, which were recast in 1913. They are considered one of the finest rings in Sussex, and can be heard over two miles away across the fields. One hundred and four neatly clipped yews are now a feature of the north and east approaches to the church, and are believed to have been planted in 1887 to mark Queen Victoria's Golden Jubilee.

In 1689 and 1764 licences were issued for a meeting of people known as 'protestant dissenters'. The Union Church of Brighton encouraged the dissenters, who outgrew their house at 4 Redbarn Cottages, behind the High Street. This house remains the home of the present administrator of the Henfield Evangelical Free Church. The dissenters were eventually able to build their chapel in 1832 on a vacant plot in the High Street. This became the Henfield Congregational Church, and the first church roll consisted of 19 members. George Hall was ordained in July 1832 and became the first

67 The Henfield Congregational Church, c.1870, showing the manse fronting the High Street. This was declared unfit for habitation and was demolished in 1904 to make way for an extension to the church. On the right is Cooper's Yard.

68 Children standing on the steps of the Nep Town Mission chapel, *c.*1910. In 1940 this joined with the Congregational Church, bringing an injection of new life and a Sunday school of 65 children. The building itself, fronting Nep Town Road, still survives as the carpentry shop of builder P.J. Luxford.

Pastor, remaining until 1871. The manse was in front of the church. Charles Tobitt, a local shopkeeper, loaned his private organ to the church and was the organist there for 55 years, during which time he missed only one service. The present organist, David Sayers, who took over from Mr Tobitt confirmed that he cannot compete with that record!

In 1901 the Rev. and Mrs Whiting came to Henfield, and within ten years the congregation had grown considerably. One of the longest pastorates in the 20th century was that of Albert Wood, who arrived in 1954 and stayed for 19 years. During that time the church enjoyed increased growth and influence in the village. The present Pastor, Graham Edwards, was appointed in 1987, and 'the church in the High Street' continues to thrive. In September 1998 a new church hall with baptistery was built at the back of the church, replacing the old hall, which had originally been a 1940s 'Prefab' house.

Tucked away in a private garden in Blackgate Lane is a second corrugated iron chapel. This was the Rehoboth Baptist Chapel. It was opened in 1897 by its first Pastor, Ebenezer Martin, who purchased the land and paid for the little chapel to be brought

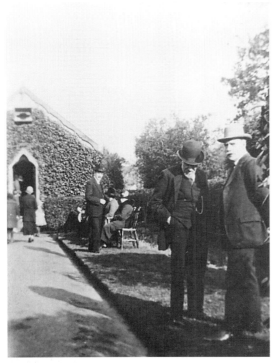

from Blackstone and re-erected in Henfield. It soon had a congregation of 50 with an active Sunday school. By the time that Mr Martin left in 1921, however, numbers had declined and, although they revived in 1963, it finally closed in 1990 and was sold.

The Roman Catholic Church of Corpus Christi was built in the grounds of Red Oaks in 1929 during the time that Mrs Lilian Stern lived there. Prior to this services had been held in her house. The original church was a wooden structure, which was replaced by the present church in 1974. The priest's house next to the church had been built in 1969, and in 1998 a new church hall was built on the site of the original church. However, the history of Roman Catholic worship in the village goes back many more years than this, for in 1889 the first training college for priests in the south of England began at Henfield Place. There has been a succession of priests at Henfield since 1931,

69   A gathering outside the Rehoboth Baptist chapel, Blackgate Lane, *c*.1900.

70   Interior of the Roman Catholic Church of Corpus Christi in 1965, after the chancel had been recessed and the inside given a coat of light-coloured paint to remove the previous dark aspect.

71 Clifton House on Henfield Common, now known as the White House. A small private school was run there, possibly by the Misses Wish in *c*.1866. The second girl from left on the back row is M. West, and fourth from left is Fanny Holman, and fifth, E. Challen. On the left of the front row is D. West, and the boy on the left is W. West. The teacher standing on the right is Miss Irish.

starting with Father Van Langendonk. Father Andrew Convey was responsible for the building of the new priest's house and new church, which were paid for by the parishioners. Nuns living at Little Whaphams south of Golden Square help prepare for the services and also take communion to the housebound.

The earliest known private school in Henfield was run by the Phillips family of Potwell between 1786 and 1806. They added a new classroom in 1788, which may be the present-day Red Oaks Lodge. In the High Street, the Misses Martin's school at Moustows Manor started in 1851 and ran for about ten years, and at Forges the Misses Harwood's School ran from *c*.1860 to *c*.1910. At Henfield Lodge in Croft Lane Edwin Churcher started his private school, known as Lucton or Henfield Grammar School in *c*.1870. This was carried on by his son, also named Edwin, until *c*.1938. In the 20th century small private schools were run by Miss Light at Chong in Upper Station Road, and by Mr and Mrs Prince in the Grey House, Cagefoot Lane.

72 Boys School on Henfield Common, *c.*1910. This closed in 1984 and is now a private house. The headmaster's house on the left was built in 1820 at a cost of £111.

Henfield was one of the first villages in West Sussex to start schools for the children of the poor. William Borrer of Barrow Hill started the 'National Society for Educating the Children of the Poor in the Principles of the Established Church' in Henfield, and persuaded residents of Henfield and surrounding villages to sponsor a pupil's education. Sixty-six did so between 1815 and 1825. The Henfield National School for Boys was established on 10 August 1812, the school room being leased from a Mr Sturt for £10 10s. a year. This may have been the classroom originally built for Phillip's School in 1788.

We know a great deal about the school in the period from 3 October 1815 to 1 August 1825, as the school register and minute book of the Society have survived. Ninety-eight pupils were admitted during the first year of the school, and 22 in the second year. Boys were admitted at six years old and left at 12 or 13 years of age. Some boys passed through the school without a gap; others were discharged and readmitted a number of times. Some left during the summer and were readmitted later in the year. The register gives the name of the boy, his age, the names and ages of his parents, their occupation, and the number of children in the family. The size of family was much larger than today, six to ten being usual. The largest family recorded was that of John and Ann Nye, glazier, who had 19 children. The fathers' occupations listed include all the trades necessary for a self-contained village, and also included two bargemen, indicating the importance of the river, the Governor of the Poorhouse, a transported convict and a tin man. The names of 25 families on the register can still be found in the village today.

Pupils had to attend school seven days a week, starting at 9 a.m. Some boys were expelled for 'irregular attendance on a Sunday', which included the morning service at St Peter's Church. The second schoolmaster, William Godley, was appointed on 5 June

1816, having gained his certificate after two months' instruction. He was still in charge of the school on his death in 1843. He was a kindly man, devoted to the boys and their education, which enabled some of them to do well in later life.

A new Boys School was built on Henfield Common at a cost of £443, and opened on 17 September 1819. This enabled a Girls School to be started in the old Boys School premises, at what is an early date for a girls school. The girls remained here until a new

73 In the centre of this photograph dating from *c.*1912 is the Girls School, which survives today as two private houses. The Donkey Field is today the site of The Hooks, an estate road leading from Broomfield Road.

74 An Infants School class in 1929 with head-mistress Miss Clara Mills, who was there from 1926-36. The school originally had one classroom, but in 1882 an extension was built on the western side to make two. In 1883 a partition was put up to divide the two classrooms, and the school remained this way until its closure.

75 The library at the Assembly Rooms was rather small and only about 2,500 books could be kept in stock at any one time. It only opened on Tuesdays, Thursdays and Saturdays.

school was built for them off Church Lane in 1834. An Infants School was built on land donated by William Borrer, next to the old workhouse in Nep Town Road, in 1844.

There is no record as to which subjects the children were taught, but great importance was placed on literacy. One school report lists the number of boys who could repeat the Lord's Prayer, the Creed, collects, graces and church catechisms. Not all the pupils could read when they left school, but those who could were given a bible. In 1824 there were 159 boys in the National School and 63 girls in the Girls School. Eight of the log books have survived. That of the Boys School for 1868 gives the subjects being taught as arithmetic, reading, spelling, transcription and composition, history, geography and religious instruction. Reasons for absence from school in the 1870s vary from osier stripping, sheep tending and driving ploughs to blackberry picking.

As the population of Henfield grew so all three schools were enlarged. In 1952 education in the area was reorganised when a new Secondary Modern School was built at Steyning. This later became a Comprehensive School, and finally combined with the old Grammar School. The Girls School closed and they joined the boys in a Mixed School on the Common. For the following year boys and girls over 11 occupied the old Girls School building as an annex to the Steyning School, after which all secondary education passed out of the village. The Infants School was in use until 1957, when a new school was opened in Fabians Way. They were joined in 1984 by the Junior Mixed School from the common. In 1999 St Peter's Church of England School was enlarged and now has a school roll of 382: 196 boys and 186 girls. There are 14 class teachers, besides the head teacher and supporting staff.

Henfield has been particularly fortunate in its choice of head teachers. As well as the long-serving Mr Godley, Cornelius Collis was head of the Boys School from 1875-1918. In the Girls School Miss Edith Hulbert was headmistress from 1907-33. Miss Eliza

Mills was head of the Infants School from 1895-1923, and Fred Cook was head of the Junior Mixed School from 1967-86.

During the 1850s there was a Mechanics Institute and library in the High Street. A public meeting was held in the Parish Room on 28 July 1925 in order to form a local branch of the County Library at Henfield. A committee was formed and Mr Hitchen was elected as honorary librarian. The library started life in the Parish Room with just over 200 books, and in March 1927 transferred to the Eardley Hall Institute, where a room was leased. This arrangement continued until February 1955 when the County Council terminated the lease. The Henfield branch library then moved to the Supper Room at the Assembly Rooms where it stayed until the present library was opened in 1970. The car park extension adjacent to the library was built in November 1971 and the library itself rebuilt and enlarged in 2000.

Over the last two centuries Henfield has had a number of family doctors; in most cases sons followed fathers. Charles Morgan and sons Frederick and Nelson, surgeons of Henfield, are mentioned on an agreement with the churchwardens and overseer of the poor in 1832, when they were appointed to care for paupers at £35 a year. During the 19th century and the first half of the 20th century there were two separate doctor's practices in Henfield. In c.1864 Dr Frederick Morgan sold his practice to Dr Charles Lewis, who built Broomfields, a purpose-built doctor's house. He was followed by his son Frederick, who on his retirement sold the practice to Dr Henry Fremlin Squire.

The other practice in the village was started by Dr Adolphus Caudle in 1834 at Elm Lodge in the High Street. He was succeeded by his son Adolphus William Wisden Caudle who, towards the end of the 19th century, went into partnership with Dr Eldon Pratt. Soon after Dr Caudle's death in 1903, Dr Pratt moved the practice to Holmwood, in the High Street, and in c.1908 it was taken over by Dr Arthur Holt.

76 Broomfields in 1961, about 10 years before it was demolished. The doctor's surgery was on the left. Squire Way now occupies the site.

77 Holmwood in the High Street in 1966, for many years the home of Dr Holt. This Edwardian building was demolished in that year to make way for the new Barclays Bank.

In those days fees were negotiable; those who could afford to pay for services did so, whilst goods were often bartered by the poor. A bale of hay or straw, or even buns collected from Cruttenden's baker's shop for Dr Lewis to eat on his round, were counted as payment for medical treatment. Before the days of the motor car, doctors visited their patients on horseback, or by pony and trap. The practices covered an area from Poynings at the foot of the South Downs to Partridge Green in the north, and included isolated farmhouses along the River Adur.

By the 1930s confinements were frequently in a nursing home, so Dr H.F. Squire started one in Haycroft, Cagefoot Lane. This was in demand until the formation of the National Health Service in 1948. Dr Squire was also a keen St John's Ambulance man; with the help of Miss Grace Barter he started first-aid classes and a division of the Brigade in Henfield.

Before 1948 home nursing was carried out by relatives or neighbours, but there was long felt to be a need for more expert nursing, so on 1 January 1888 the 'Henfield Benefit Association for Nursing the Sick' was founded. Nurse Thompson was appointed at a salary of 17s. 8d. for two weeks. She was followed by Nurse Thrift, appointed in 1897, who continued for 16 years. The costs of running the Nursing Association were met partly from annual subscriptions, which were 3s. per annum in 1932, rising to 6s. 6d. in 1944. There were also modest payments for nursing, double being charged for non-members. Continual fund-raising by the village was also necessary; concerts, fêtes, plays, baby shows and flower shows all played their part, and support was also gained from St Peter's Church. On 18 July 1913 Nurse Wooller, a lady much loved and appreciated by the village, was appointed, and she remained a district nurse and midwife for 30 years. Under the 1948 National Health Act, West Sussex County Council became responsible for district nurses. The assets of the Nursing Association were then used for grocery vouchers and help with heating for the sick and elderly, until it was finally wound up after 100 years.

During the Second World War Dr H.F. Squire was called up into the RAF as a medical officer, as was his son John, who qualified as a doctor in 1942. In their absence the practice was continued by retired medic Dr Garrett with help from Mrs Squire and the dispenser Miss Grace Barter. After the war Dr John Squire purchased Dr Holt's practice, thus uniting the two of them. At first he used Dr Holt's surgery, which had a small unheated consulting room. The waiting room had only two wooden chairs, but it was unusual then to see more than five or six patients during a surgery, there being no appointments. Later Woodlawn, Cagefoot Lane was purchased. This had a stable block which could be converted into a surgery, and was used as such for 24 years. After the National Health Act Dr H.F. Squire took only private patients, whilst Dr John Squire joined the National Health Service. Later Dr H.F.'s health deteriorated and

78   When appointed, Nurse Wooller was given a furnished cottage, seen here in the background, by J.E. Hall, and a salary of £60 a year. It was not until 1916 that a bicycle was bought for her. Later she used a motor cycle, and finally a motor car to do her rounds. On the left is Tannery Cottage, and on the right the Cat House.

79 The surgery at Wood-lawn, Cagefoot Lane in the 1960s. Dr John Squire opened his surgery in January 1948. In 1952 an old garage at the side was converted into a second consulting room.

assistants were needed, and when Henfield began to grow in the 1950s Dr Paul Wellings joined the partnership. A new surgery was built on land belonging to Woodlawn, opening onto Hewitts. This building, known as the Health Centre, was opened in 1971, and gradually more partners joined. These included Dr Robin Norman, Dr Anna Haylett, Dr Malcolm McLean, Dr Patrick Reade and others. As the practice grew it became possible to take on a nurse, and Patricia Bedwell joined in 1969 and stayed for 27 years.

After the Health Centre was taken over by the District Health Authority, money was always short and even repairs were not carried out. The doctors decided that the only solution was to build their own, larger surgery. A site was found at the northern edge of Henfield, adjacent to the proposed new housing development at Parsonage Farm. There was only sufficient funding for the actual construction of the building, so Dr Reade and the 'Friends of the Medical Centre' set to work fund-raising in order to equip it. The building opened in 1994 and shortly afterwards was extended to provide a well-used physiotherapy room.

Before 1894, annual vestry meetings, when the churchwardens and overseers of the poor were elected, had to be called by the church and these were responsible for running the village's affairs. In the 1890s the Liberal government led by William Gladstone wished to revitalise parishes on more democratic lines, which resulted in the formation of parish councils. Throughout the country each parish had to hold a meeting on 4 December 1894, and all those with more than 300 inhabitants had to form a council. If more than the required number of candidates were nominated, then an election had to be held on 17 December. The Electoral Register of Henfield for 1894 contained the names of 298 men and 18 women, as not everybody was entitled to vote, and the first Parish Council meeting was held at 7 p.m. on 2 January 1895 in the Infants School. The letter inviting the new councillors to attend was signed by the chairman of the Parish Meeting, Henry West of Terry's Cross, Woodmancote, who was later elected as first Chairman of the Council, a post he held for ten years.

The new Council took over all the non-ecclesiastical powers and duties of the Vestry Committee. Initially, it had very little income. In 1895 the poor rate for general purposes was £80, but it varied from year to year, being £40 in 1897 and only £8 in 1899. The clerk's annual salary was £15 until 1918, when it was raised to £20. All capital expenditure in the village had to be raised on loans to be paid back over 20-30 years. In 1884 the Church Vestry had taken out a loan of £600 to purchase and lay out a new burial ground. This was taken over by the Parish Council, who took out further loans

80 Results of the 1894 Parish Council election. Henfield's first elected Parish Council consisted of the vicar, two doctors, four farmers, two builders, a butcher, a grocer, and three land owners, a good democratic mixture of residents.

ELECTION OF PARISH COUNCILLORS

For the Parish [or for the _____ Ward of the Parish] of Henfield in the Year 1894.

DECLARATION OF RESULT OF POLL.

I, THE UNDERSIGNED, being the Deputy Returning Officer [or Deputy Returning Officer duly authorised in that behalf] at the Poll for the Election of Parish Councillors for the said Parish [or Ward] held on the 17th day of DECEMBER, 1894, DO HEREBY GIVE NOTICE that the number of Votes recorded for each Candidate at the Election is as follows:—

Surnames	Other Names	Places of Abode	Number of Votes recorded
Beckett	Thomas	Henfield	68
Brooks	William	Hole Dean	151
Brunning	Frederick Charles	Church Street	53
Caudle	Adolphus Will. Wisden	Henfield	69
Dunlop	Charles Seward	Red Oaks	92
Edwards	George	Nursery	51
Evans	Joshua	The Lodge, Parsonage farm	41
Frost	James William	Glenavon	76
Gravely	Arthur	Henfield	68
Greenfield	James	High Street	143
Hall	John Eardley	Barrow Hill	107
Heaver	Charles Champion	Kentons	108
Johnson	Joseph	High Street	46
King	William	New Inn	66
Lewis	Charles Francis	Broomfields	162
Lewis	Frederick	Broomfields	93
Longley	Henry	Henfield	36
Martin	James	Henfield	81
Musson	John Thomas	High Street	80
Roberts	George	Hill Side	119
Roberts	William	7 South View Terrace	80
Rowland	Frederick	The Nurseries	21
Smith	Charles	Whaphams	104
Standen	John	East House	144
Stevens	James Waller	Henfield	115
Thorns	Thomas	Henfield	143
Tobitt	John	High Street	60
Tobitt	Samuel	Russ House	112
Vinall	George	Nep Town	143
Wadey	Alfred	Nep Town	
Weller	James Milford	Broadmere common	

And I DO HEREBY DECLARE that the said C. F. Lewis, W. Brooks, J. Standen, J. Greenfield, T. Thorns, G. Roberts, J. Stevens, S. Tobitt, C. Smith, C. Heaver J. C. Hall. F. Lewis, C. S. Dunlop, J. Martin.

J. Musson } are to be decided
W. Roberts }

are duly Elected PARISH COUNCILLORS for the said Parish [or Ward]. the election failing for the ...

Dated this 17th day of DECEMBER, 1894.

C. Shackleton _____ Returning Officer.

Parish Councillors Election Order, 1894.
First Sched., Form No. 6.   * Add "Deputy" here, if the Declaration is signed by the Deputy Returning Officer.

(P. C. Elec. 31 in List.)—Printed and Published by HADDEN, BEST & Co., West Harding Street, London, E.C.

of £250 and £350 in 1907 when the cemetery was extended to two and a quarter acres. Under the Burial Act, parishes received additional sums, which in 1895 amounted to £50.

The work of the Parish Council was divided among committees. At first the Burial Committee was the most active, but in 1907-8 the Water Committee became very involved with providing mains water to many of the cottages. Mains water became available in the village in 1902 when a supply was obtained from the Steyning Water Works Company at Upper Beeding. Some gas lights had been installed by the Vestry Committee, but the Parish Council extended the lighting in 1912, and these lamps continued in use until 1932 when superseded by electric lighting.

The Parish Council is now responsible for public open spaces including the 'Kings Field' recreation ground to the north of Upper Station Road. The field was given to the village by Miss Margaret Knowles of Henfield Place to mark the Silver Jubilee of King George V in 1935. The field originally bounded Upper Station Road, but in the 1960s houses were built along the road, and additional land was acquired at the side and adjacent to the school to compensate. The first play equipment to be installed in the Kings Field was swings, a slide and a sand pit. Today there is much more equipment and a designated area for young children to play in. In 1990, with the help of grants from Horsham District Council, the Henfield and District Sports Centre was built next to the Kings Field.

81 The Lych Gate at Henfield Cemetery, *c.*1890. The oak gates were made and erected by William Ward, the local builder, in 1885 at a cost of £7.

In the 1960s Chanctonbury Rural District Council first began to consult its parish councils about planning applications. At first the Chairman and Vice Chairman dealt with them, but a Plans Advisory Committee was later formed. This committee now deals with about 140 planning applications a year, working hard to preserve the many listed buildings and to ensure that development is in keeping with the scale of the village. The Parish Council has managed Henfield Common, Oreham Common, Broadmere Common, Hundred Steddle Waste and Mock Bridge Green since the 1940s. To them has now been added the Tanyard Field in the centre of the village.

82 The Henfield Fire Brigade attending a fire at Blackstone, *c.*1910. It was not uncommon at this time for the brigade to arrive too late to save the property. Nonetheless, they seem proud of their efforts! In the foreground, from left to right: E.L. Merrett, W. Heasman, W.A. Powell.

Henfield is one of only a few Parish Councils to have its own coat of arms. It was granted on 3 March 1992, the scheme being initiated and financed by Father Mark Elvins, with Peter Hudson, Chairman of the Parish Council negotiating with the College of Arms for approval. A Henfield artist, Brenda Hobbs, designed the coat of arms. The main charge of the Henfield shield is the arms of the Bysshopp family, who lived in the village in the 16th and 17th centuries, with the crossed keys of St Peter. The pelican in her piety symbolises the Roman Catholic Church of Corpus Christi. The crest of a golden oriole on a thorn bush commemorates William Borrer, whose son claimed to have seen 14 golden orioles on Henfield Common. The motto *Domine Salva Nos* [Lord save us] is the family motto of the Elvins family.

In 1904 a fire brigade was formed, run by a committee of the Parish Council, and in April it was proposed that a 'fire appliance be supplied for extinguishing fires'. The original appliance was a hand cart with hoses which was kept in Mr Tobitt's coach house, at Magnolia House in the High Street, at a rent of £6 per annum. The first captain of the fire brigade was Allan Baxter, a position he held at Henfield for 36 years until his retirement in 1940. The only villages in the area to have fire brigades at an earlier date were Hurstpierpoint and Steyning.

In 1906 a horse-drawn manual Merryweather fire engine was presented to the village by John Eardley Hall of Barrow Hill. The handcart was sold for £1 10s. It took a minimum of five men each side of the engine to operate the pump, for which they were paid 6d. an hour. The two horses used to draw the engine belonged to Bill Shepherd, a local fly proprietor, and were kept in *The George* yard. In later years the appliance was pulled behind a builder's lorry. Each fireman had a white enamelled sign on his gate with 'Fireman' boldly written in red. It was the job of 'call boys' on their bicycles to alert the firemen when the alarm was raised. In 1907 Mr Hall provided a fire bell for the station; later there was a klaxon horn on a shed at Henfield Motors. In August 1934 the Parish Council took out a loan of £300 to purchase a second-hand 1915 Dennis fire engine from West Sussex County Council, and the manual fire engine was sold for £2, the harness fetching £1 10s. It was at this time that the fire station was moved from the coach house to its present site just south of Golden Square. In *c.*1950, when the 1915 Dennis fire engine was replaced by a new appliance, a larger station was built on the side of the existing one.

'Joe' Gillett joined the fire brigade in 1935 and served for 32 years, 17 as Station Officer. During his tenure Henfield won the cup for the most efficient part-time station in West Sussex, and were runners-up on a number of occasions. During the war years the work of the fire brigade greatly increased, and to meet the demand an auxiliary fire crew was formed, increasing the number of firemen to twenty-three. Henfield Parish Council continued to run the brigade until 1942, when it was taken over first by Chanctonbury Rural District Council and, in 1948, by West Sussex County Council. Some statements of accounts for the fire brigade survive; charges were made for putting out fires. In 1913 receipts for attending fires amounted to £12 12s. and payments for fire service, £35 10s. 3d. There also survives correspondence from a lady who felt that she had been overcharged for putting out her chimney fire.

In 1908 Captain Baxter, a keen first-aider, suggested to the Parish Council that they should obtain a wheeled stretcher for use in the village. A concert was held to raise the money and a one-man ambulance was purchased for £16 7s. 3d. in 1909. This was kept in the fire station, was last used in about 1932 to convey a lady who had collapsed in Station Road to her home in West End Lane, and is now in the Museum. The need for an ambulance club was recognised by Dr H.F. Squire and J.A. Brazier, and this resulted in the 'Henfield and District Ambulance Club' being formed by R.B. Rann and others in February 1934. For an annual subscription of 1s. 6d. the club provided a round the clock ambulance service for its members who at the end of the first year of operation were 699 in number.

In 1937 the original ambulance was replaced by a newer and larger converted saloon car, which served the club until March 1944, when a second-hand two-stretcher ambulance was purchased for £650. When the 1947 Health Act came into force on 5 July 1948 the club elected to cease operations and in accordance with the trust deed, which had been set up to cover the vehicle, this was handed over to the St John Ambulance Brigade who acted as agents for West Sussex County Council. The ambulance continued to be based in Henfield until 1963, when it was moved to Worthing.

83 The Fire Brigade in 1937 with the 1915 Dennis engine. On the machine, left to right: A. Reeves, Capt. Allan Baxter, Reg Gander, Bill Parsons, Bill Watts, Fred Ruff, Tom Thorns; Standing, from left to right: Vic Parsons, George Chowne, Ike Dale, Frank Clarke, 'Joe' Gillett.

84 J.A. Brazier and his sister with the first ambulance, photographed on Henfield Common in May 1935.

85   Henfield Parish Council, 1965. Standing from left to right: Ken Jones; Brig. H. Mosley; Donald Whittome; Dr John Squire; Eric Whittome, O.B.E.; Air Cdr. John Freeman, C.B.E.; Benson Coleman. Seated around the table: 'Joe' Gillett; Mrs F. Segre (deputy clerk); G.W. Somerville, O.B.E. (clerk); F.J.R. Dodd; Mrs A. Blair-Fish; Percy Groves; Mrs M. Peters; Adm. Sir Geoffrey Oliver. In front of the table: Lucie Bishop. Members of the press including Jimmie Armour-Milne and Barbara Rhys are at the table on the left.

The Henfield Assembly Rooms Company was formed in 1885 for the purpose of purchasing a site in the High Street, the erection of a building, and its maintenance. Construction began at once, the contractors being Birdhead Brothers of Partridge Green. From its layout it appears that the building was designed with the intention of housing occasional Masonic functions. Although the company was founded with a nominal capital of 1,700 £1 shares, only 137 were sold. The founder shareholders were Dr C.F. Lewis, Richard Hales of Woodmancote Rectory, Charles Aubrey Wade, solicitor, Henry Longley, draper, Matthew Neale, chemist, William West, assistant overseer and Stephen Caudle, Esquire. By July 1885 £559 had been raised, but in October 1887 the building had to be mortgaged. By 1890 the £1 shares had risen to £803, but this sum was never exceeded. Debts continued to mount, rising to £2,024 in 1910, and by 1919 the debt of the mortgagees was in excess of the sale value of the building.

Despite these financial troubles the village enjoyed the use of the building, it being much larger than the three school halls which had previously been used for functions. On 27 January 1887 a Choral Society concert was held, and the new rooms became the centre for most village events for the next 87 years. The Parish Council proceeded to use the small front room as a clerk's office, the 'Supper Room' for the quarterly Council meetings, and the large hall for the annual parish meeting. In the 1890s the Council paid the Assembly Rooms Company £5 a year for this.

In 1921 Henfield Parish Council took out a loan of £1,800 to purchase the Assembly Rooms, which had by this time become dilapidated through years of neglect. £270 was spent on repairs and furnishings. They provided the Council with a parish office, two halls, one with a stage and dressing rooms, a kitchen, caretaker's cottage and income from rental. The Assembly Rooms were back in business again, and much money was invested in maintaining the rooms, and installing electricity, heating and a dance floor. At one time the Registrar had his office here, and the postmen used part of it as a temporary sorting office at Christmas time.

By the early 1960s Eric Whittome, Chairman of the Parish Council, reported that there were difficulties in maintaining the Assembly Rooms, mainly due to cost, and something larger was required. During 1966 a committee carefully considered 12 different sites, and with hindsight it is clear that a good decision was made to build the new Village Hall on Greenfield's market garden behind *The George Hotel* in the High Street. The site was large enough to build a hall complex capable of future expansion, an office for the Parish Council, a museum, a garden at the rear and a large car park in front.

The planning sub-committee started its work in August 1971, under the chairmanship of Ian Varley, who remained Chairman for six years. The village then began years of fund-raising. Planning permission was granted in November 1972, subject to suitable access being available, but it was not until 1977 that the Post Office released land at Coopers Yard for an access road, so there were several years without a proper car park. It was essential to begin building in 1973 because of rising costs, and as the hall began to take shape the many societies that would be using it donated fittings and furniture, among them the Women's Institute, who donated £2,000 to equip the kitchen.

The Village Hall finally opened on 11 November 1974 with a whole day of celebrations. Henfield became the envy of surrounding villages with its large hall, seating 300 with stage and lighting, small hall and committee room. In 1975 the old Assembly Rooms were sold and converted into three shops with accommodation above and at the rear. That building still retains some of its original façade and the original clock face, although the workings of the clock are now in Henfield Museum. By 1993 it was evident that the museum and Parish Council office were too small, and the entrance foyer of the Village Hall was inadequate for large functions, so the front part of the building was rebuilt. This provided both a larger museum and office, and improved access and facilities for the Village Hall. The complex is now known as The Henfield Hall, the largest room being named the Whittome Hall. In 2000 another hall was added to the rear, forming the Garden Suite, and the kitchen was enlarged.

The Parish Council Museum started with the private collection of Miss Alice Standen in the 1920s. This was added to by her niece, Miss Lucie Bishop, a long-serving parish and district councillor. By 1948 a large collection of domestic bygones, costumes, paintings, photographs, farm implements, etc. had been gathered, and this was housed in two

86 Speeches at the opening of the new Village Hall in 1974. On the stage from left to right: Mr Allerton (architect); Dr John Squire; Sir Peter Mursell; Eric Whittome; Lady Mursell.

87 Miss Lucie Bishop, Chairman of the Museum Committee, in Henfield Museum as it was between 1974 and 1993. She was also a member of Chanctonbury Rural District Council and West Sussex County Council for many years. In the foreground is the one-man ambulance.

cupboards on the upstairs landing in the Assembly Rooms. A Museum Committee was then formed to sort out and administer the collection. In 1951, to mark the Festival of Britain, the Museum Committee organised an exhibition on 13 and 14 August in the Boys School on the common. This illustrated the history and development of Henfield from early times, and the industries and arts and crafts of the day, and this was a great success. Villagers lent objects, some of which were later donated to the collection.

By the time that the new Village Hall opened the collection had grown sufficiently to fill a new room, and Henfield finally had its own Museum. Wooden showcases were obtained from Bognor Regis Museum, and the collection was laid out by the Museum Committee under the chairmanship of 'Joe' Gillett. Larger objects which had been stored in various locations could now be displayed for the first time. These included a 'penny farthing' bicycle made by William Powell, and the one-man ambulance. The walls were lined with the large collection of local paintings and photographs. Uniforms of the Henfield branch of the Sussex Rifle Volunteers, dresses that Henfield ladies would have worn in Edwardian times, domestic bygones, farm tools, local fossils and prehistoric flint tools completed the displays. 'Joe' Gillett opened the present museum in 1994.

Five

HENFIELD AT WAR

DURING THE ENGLISH CIVIL WAR, which began in 1642 and finally finished with the Battle of Worcester in 1651, battle raged at Arundel, only 20 miles away, where the castle was sacked in 1644. Although Henfield seems to have survived intact, and St Peter's Church shows no signs of having been visited by the destructive 'levellers', loyalties in the village were divided.

On 25 February 1641, 166 males over 18 years of age were forced to sign the 'Protestation commanded by the Commons House of Parliament'. This was effectively the first census in Henfield. King Charles I had imposed unpopular taxes and was, it was claimed, being influenced by the Roman Catholic Church. Parliament was insisting on adherence to the Protestant faith. The protestation reads: 'I ... do in the presence of Almighty God, promise, vow and protest, to maintain and defend, as far as lawfully with my life, power, and estate the true Reformed Protestant Religion expressed in the doctrine of the Church of England'.

The first to sign were the vicar, John Goldsmith, the 'cunstable' Edward Boniface, the churchwardens Henry Bysshopp and 'Nocolas Gallope', and the 'overseers of the poore' William Woolgar and Tho. Livinge, who took an oath in front of Henry Goringe, 'His Majesties Justice of the Peace'. Then follow the signatures or marks of the other men of the village, and there were none recorded that did not sign the Protestation. Among them are the names of some present-day Henfield residents: Baker, Cannon, Chaete, Davy, Goffe, Greenfield, Hayne, Hills, Holden, Holney, Jupe, Morley, Page, Parson, Stokes, Vinall and White. Also signing was Prosper Rainsford, who, as we have seen, had been a courtier of Charles I. There would not be another census in Henfield for 160 years.

Despite having signed the Protestation, Henry Bysshopp, who lived at Parsonage House in Church Street, was a loyal supporter of the King and, having fought in the Battle of Arundel when Roundheads came to arrest him, he avoided capture by hiding with his dog in a secret hiding place in his house. He then left for America and spent two years in Virginia, where he had earlier bought some land. When he returned he had to make his peace with Parliament.

88   Parsonage House in Church Street, *c*.1914, once the home of Henry Bysshopp.

During the Commonwealth period the church lost much of its property, as did many supporters of the King, including Henry Bysshopp. The Manor of Stretham was confiscated and sold to Colonel John Downes, M.P. for Arundel, although many of the tenants remained the same. In order to have an accurate valuation of these properties, a 'Survey of the Manor of Stretham, Henfield' was made in 1647. This is a long, detailed account of all the boundaries of the manor, the properties in it, to whom they were leased, and their value. Many of the properties mentioned are familiar to us today, including: 'Barrow Hill, Batts, Great Betley, Buskwish [Buckwish Farm], Catsland, Eatons, Lashmarshall, Lipride, New Hall, Parsonage House, Pokelye [Pokerlee Farm], Potwell, Staples'. The manor farmhouse of Stretham was in the hands of Thomas Bellingham, who is recorded as having been with Charles I at Oxford in 1641, whilst New Hall was occupied by Prosper Rainsford's son George.

The survey describes the customs of the parish, and mentions that: 'There are two fayres a year, one upon Saint George's Day at Henfield Towne and uppon Henfield Common and the other upon Saint Margaret's Day at Pillory Greene'. The pillory and stocks were in the High Street opposite the blacksmiths. The field on the south side of Cagefoot Lane, where one fair was held, was still being used for village functions up until the early 20th century. At the restoration of the monarchy, Downes was executed as a regicide, having been one of the signatories of the King's death warrant, and the manor was returned to the Bishop of Chichester.

Throughout the 18th and 19th centuries there were periodic scares about invasion by the French. Longley Brothers in the High Street made the scarlet uniforms for the Henfield Rifle Volunteers in the 19th century, examples of which are in Henfield Museum. The volunteer movement was set up in this country in the 1850s because it was realised that the regular army was not large enough to defend the country should it come under attack from the French. It took the form of either rifle or artillery volunteers.

89 *The White Hart Inn* in Henfield High Street, where the 1647 survey of the manor of Stretham was compiled. It is seen here in *c.*1885, when it was owned by the West family.

90   Dr C.F. Lewis of 'Broomfields', at camp in Arundel Park, *c*.1890. He became the Honorary Assistant Surgeon in the Rifle Volunteers in 1866 and retired in 1897 as a Brigadier Surgeon Lieutenant Colonel.

In 1860 Henfield became the 18th Corps of rifle volunteers to be raised in Sussex, and in 1861 they became part of the 2nd Administrative Battalion Sussex Rifle Volunteers. Further reorganisations followed in 1871 and in 1880, when they became 'L' Company 2nd Sussex Rifle Volunteers. Initially each corps had a choice of either green, dark grey or scarlet for their uniforms, but from 1880 only scarlet was used. Prominent local people became involved with the volunteers. Dr A.W.W. Caudle from Elm Lodge in the High Street became a surgeon-lieutenant in 1878 and retired in 1889. The Rev. John O'Brien, who was vicar of Henfield for 21 years, was honorary chaplain from 1861 until his death in 1872. Henry T. West of Terry's Cross was appointed captain in 1885, and honorary major in 1888, and retired in 1891. The sergeant instructor from 1873-87 was W. Swingler, formerly of the Coldstream Guards, who used to live in the High Street opposite St Anthony's Cottage. Rifle practice was carried out at the ranges at Steyning. George Roberts, a local builder and water diviner who lived at Hillside at the top of Windmill Lane, was a sergeant. William Woodard, son of Nathaniel Woodard was a captain between 1873 and 1879. At the time of the Great War the rifle volunteers were integrated with the Royal Sussex Regiment.

A small number of local men fought in the Boer Wars, and Gunner Scutt, Capt. Harold Thorns, Major Leslie Thorns, Major A.G. Wade, and Private Woolgar all arrived home safely afterwards. In 1901 Brigadier General J.R.P. Gordon of Moustows Manor arrived back in Henfield on sick leave and was escorted from the station to his home by a procession led by the village band. In the early years of the 20th century the Sussex Yeomanry and Territorial Army, based at Brighton, came to camp at Henfield in the field now occupied by the northern end of Furners Mead. Seeing the soldiers in the village encouraged a number of young men to join the territorials around 1911.

91   The Sussex Yeomanry at summer camp in *c.*1910 in the field which now forms the northern end of Furners Mead. In the centre distance is Backsettown.

92 Local recruits to the Territorial Army outside the Assembly Rooms in *c*.1912. Sitting on the nearside of the carriage at the rear is Harold Cruttenden, and next to him is John Alliss. Both lost their lives in the First World War. Sitting on the offside, fourth from left, is Tom Page.

Soon after war was declared in 1914 a Civil Guard similar to the later Home Guard was formed, comprising approximately 40 men trained by Sergeant Swingler. In 1917 they had to guard a British aeroplane which had been forced to land with engine trouble at Backsettown, until it was transported back to Shoreham Airfield on a lorry the next day. Many local horses were commandeered for the war, including those stabled at the *White Hart* for the Vanderbilt coach.

Great efforts were made during the war to increase food production because of the blockade of Britain by the German navy. As soon as it was formed in Henfield in 1917, the W.I. made food production its priority. They cultivated a piece of land given by Mr Bishop to grow vegetables, and applied to the copyholders of Henfield Common to be allowed to graze goats on the common. They also started rabbit and pig clubs and sold their produce at a weekly market held in the twitten at the side of *The Plough Inn*.

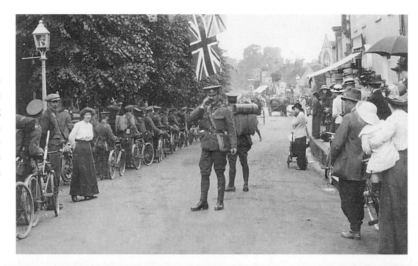

93 The 24th Division of the Cycle Corps were billeted at houses in Henfield during 1915. They are seen here in the High Street outside the Assembly Rooms about to leave for the station to catch a train to the south coast.

94 Members of the W.I. at Parsonage Farm in 1918, being given instruction by the young lady in the centre of the front row in cheese making. Second from the left in the front row is Alice Standen, treasurer of the W.I. at the time, and the first woman to serve on Henfield Parish Council, being elected in 1919.

95 The Peace Day procession on 19 July 1919, passing through the High Street on the way to Henfield Common where a 'Drum Head' service was held, followed by sports for all ages, a tea for the old folks, and, in the evening, dancing followed by a firework display and singing.

The Assembly Rooms were put to good use during the war, becoming the base for the Voluntary Aid Detachment of nurses, and the War Work Depot which was run by Miss Knowles for its three and a half years' existence. The women involved made over 2,000 items of clothing which were sent overseas to the troops. In September 1918 the Assembly Rooms were used to house German prisoners-of-war for the winter. Barbed wire was put across the windows, and guards were housed in the caretaker's cottage. During the summer the prisoners had camped in the Millfield and worked on the market gardens.

Although an armistice was declared on 11 November 1918, the peace treaty was not signed and ratified until 28 June 1919. Peace celebrations took place in Henfield on 19 July, 21 July and 4 August. These comprised sports on Henfield Common, which included a race from Partridge Green Station to Henfield, tea parties for young and old, a firework display, concerts and a cricket match.

The tremendous loss of life during the war was felt in towns and villages up and down the country and Henfield was no exception. Some 60 young men from the parish lost their lives and others returned home wounded or without limbs. The war killed virtually a generation of young men and led to great social change in the country. Afterwards there was a need for houses, so in the 1920s more were built in Upper Station Road west of Faircox Lane. The land on the southern side had been sold off as building plots back in 1912. Council houses tend to be built on the periphery of villages, and the first in Henfield were built at Hollands Road c.1922, followed in 1927 by houses in Hollands Lane and West End Lane. These had bathrooms and provided a better standard of accommodation than many of the old workers' cottages around the village. This was reflected in the rental, which at 8s. 6d. per week was twice that being paid by people in some of the old cottages.

Towards the end of the 1930s the country was again preparing itself for war. The excavation of the sandpit to the west of Southview Terrace had been completed by 1938, no doubt to meet the demand for civil defence works and sand bags. Concrete pill boxes were constructed to protect the railway bridges over the River Adur at Stretham and Betley, and also Mock Bridge. Brick air-raid shelters were built around the village,

96 The unveiling and dedication of the War Memorial outside the 'Comrades Club' on 17 June 1923. Mrs Miller unveiled the memorial and Capt. Miller placed the first wreath on behalf of the Henfield Branch of the Royal British Legion.

97 Hollands Road council houses under construction, *c.*1920. Alfred Baigent the builder is the man on the right wearing a bowler hat; next to him is Bill Browning. Holding the horse in the centre of the photograph is Harry Matthews Snr. and standing on the left is Alfred Farrell.

98 Albert Baker with R.O.C. equipment in 1925. This is an early Marjorie Baker photograph, originally entitled 'a watcher of the sky'.

including three on the Rothery field and two at the back of the Common which were eventually demolished by the Territorial Army in 1965. The middle of the three on the Rothery field was retained and extended, and used as a changing room for the football club until the new pavilion was opened in 1995. There are still a few shelters surviving around the village today such as the one at the western end of Park Road.

By the time that war was declared, on 3 September 1939, organisations such as the Civil Defence, Women's Voluntary Service (W.V.S.), Special Police and Royal Observer Corps (R.O.C.) had been in place for a number of years. In fact the R.O.C. had had a post at Henfield since 1925 on the market garden behind *The George Hotel*. In 1942 it was moved to a site in Stonepit Lane, just west of Stonepit House, which gave much better all-round visibility. In charge of the post was Albert Baker, a local butcher. The R.O.C. post was later moved to a field just to the north of Furners Farm, and continued operations into the 1960s. To combat possible German invasion, the Henfield and Woodmancote Local Defence Volunteers were formed in May 1940. Some 100 men made up the company, whose primary role in the event of invasion was to defend the road junction at Golden Square. Mrs Dorothy Squire, wife of Dr H.F. Squire, was appointed to run the local W.V.S. in January 1939. They were responsible for, among other things, housing evacuees, war savings, staffing the control room, office duties, sewing and knitting for the troops, helping with school dinners and land work. Evacuees began arriving at Henfield in early September 1939 and this continued until at least 1943. Any house that had spare rooms had to take in evacuees. The children were divided between the three village schools and they brought a teacher with them. Contingency plans were put in place in 1941 to evacuate 230 people to Henfield from the coastal towns if it was felt that an invasion was imminent.

As in the First World War, the W.I. concentrated on food production and providing clothing for, amongst others, victims of bombing. During the war some 2,214 articles of clothing were knitted by the W.I.'s handicraft guild, 1,757 lb. of jam was made and

99 The Henfield and Woodmancote Home Guard in May 1941 in the garden of Springhills at the top of Barrow Hill. Sixth from left in the second row is D.M. Sandbach and seventh is George Rothery who were Woodmancote and Henfield section leaders.

100   Special Constables in 1943 included some of the local businessmen. Fifth from left in the back row is V. Musson, sixth is W. Brunning, and seventh J. Bowden. In the middle row on left is G. Banfield and next to him A. Betchley. Police Constable White is in the centre.

12,329 cans of fruit and tomatoes sealed, nearly three quarters of a ton of rose hips were collected, and 1,274 pies made and distributed for farm workers. In the 'Dig for Victory' campaign much land in the village was given over to allotments including the strip on the west side of Hay Croft in Cagefoot Lane. Allotments also existed on the field immediately north of Henfield Place and on the site of Nep Close. The inaugural meeting of the Henfield Village Produce Association, formed to promote the growing of food and the keeping of animals to help the war effort, took place on 6 October 1942, and was chaired by Commander Block. Their first produce stall was set up in *The Plough* yard by the Misses Harcourt-Vernon in 1944.

In August 1940 the first bombs were dropped locally, landing on Shermanbury and very close to the railway line at Stretham Bridge. Bombs were dropped close to the village, the railway line being an obvious target, but the village itself escaped any direct hits. Incendiary bombs landed on the village in October 1940, however, causing fires at 'Acacia' and Hay Croft in Cagefoot Lane. Conventional bombing raids were continued until the early part of 1944, after which V1 flying bombs or 'doodlebugs' were used until November 1944. The only local fatality was a girl killed by shrapnel in New Hall Lane in October 1940, when some 40 other properties in the area received damage.

So as not to attract the attention of enemy aeroplanes when the sun or moon shone on it, the weathercock on the church tower was removed for the duration of the war. During the Battle of Britain locals had to beware of stray bullets from 'dog fights' taking place overhead. A Spitfire on a test flight was shot down locally in 1940. The wounded pilot landed on the brooks and the aeroplane crashed just west of Paynesfield on the Albourne Road. In 1943 most of the aircrew 'baled out' from a Halifax bomber in difficulties just to the west of the village. The pilot, however, stayed on board and made a forced landing at Epsom. In May 1944 emergency landing strips were constructed in a field between Park Farm and Chess Bridge, and in a field to the west of Woods Mill, but only one aeroplane is known to have made use of them.

During the war every effort was made to keep village life as normal as possible. In December 1939 the Boys School choir went around the village carol singing, which raised £5 1s. 9d., of which £3 went to school funds and the rest to good causes. The Junior Imperial League ('Imps'), who had reformed during the war as the 'Hilarity Club' put on performances in the Parish Room and the Assembly Rooms. The Henfield Players also managed to put on a number of shows despite many of its members being on active service. Proceeds from the events went to the Red Cross and other charities. All sorts of entertainments and fund-raising events were put on in aid of charity, such

101 Members of the Decontamination and Rescue Party in 1944. On left of the third row is Bill Goacher. The left of the second row is J. Curd, and fourth from left is P. Brooks the butcher. Second from left on the front row is S. Austin, fourth from left is R. Knapp, and far right is F. Wenham.

as music recitals, garden parties, fêtes, dances and whist drives. Even the Home Guard staged the pantomime 'Cinderella' in April 1942. The Girls' Friendly Society put on entertainments and sold handmade toys to raise money for the 'Aid to China Fund' and overseas missionary work.

Money subscribed locally for the National Savings Campaign always exceeded the targets set by the District Council. For the 'Salute the Soldier Week' campaign in 1944, £42,500 was raised, £17,500 above the target figure. The right-hand window of the Post Office was given over to displays for National Savings Week campaigns. For the 'War Weapons Week' campaign in December 1940, the display was of a harbour and ships. Local artists Malcolm and Hilda Milne of 'Dykes' produced the artwork and 17-year-old David Thorns made the harbour and model ships. A battleship acted as a pointer to the amount of money raised.

Cricket continued to be played during the war, with servicemen billeted in the village sometimes being called upon to make up the numbers. Canadian soldiers were billeted at Barrow Hill, Martyn Lodge and The Pools. American and British troops were also stationed in the village. It was the Canadians who built the block houses around the village and gun emplacements behind *The George Hotel*, at South View Terrace and by the windmill on the Lydds. Many of the soldiers who frequented *The George Hotel* carved their names on the exposed timber beams in the bar. This idea was started by a Bud Rogers of Dallas, Texas, and in the end there were over 5,000 names on the beams. Some of the G.I.s courted local girls and at least seven got married and left the village to start a new life in the U.S.A. or Canada.

Part of the Girls School was given over to a rest centre and store for emergency equipment and rations which in 1942 comprised 48 12 oz. tins of meat, 24 tins of syrup, 24 lb. of cocoa and sugar and 48 tins of unsweetened milk. As well as working on the market gardens German P.O.W.s made wooden toys which they sold to buy cigarettes. Not all of them wished to be repatriated after the war, and some married local girls and stayed in Britain. A TocH canteen for the troops was set up in the upstairs of the Eardley Hall Institute. One of the founders of TocH during the Great War, Bishop Neville Talbot, died at Backsettown in April 1939 where he had been recuperating from a heart attack. The TocH branch at Henfield was formed in 1933 and closed in 1947.

Henfield was allocated an air-raid siren at the beginning of the war which was sited at Betchley's garage in the High Street. It was only used about half a dozen times before local objections stopped its use. The Air Raid Precautions (A.R.P.) wardens and others were notified when enemy aircraft were coming by young men who acted as messengers. Betchley's garage became a factory during wartime where some 28 women made fuel tanks for spitfires and carried out other munitions work. May Morey, who had had previous experience with war work in her father's workshop, had the job of inspecting the quality of the work being produced.

As the war came to an end, local operations were scaled down. In December 1944 the Home Guard had its 'stand down' parade, and from March 1945 the A.R.P. post at the Assembly Rooms closed down during day time. January 1945 saw the street lamps lit again for the first time since the blackout. A committee under the chairmanship of S.G. Wright organised the V.E. Day celebrations which took place between 8 and 10 May 1945. On 10 May Mr Pound and his staff from the Boys School organised a children's sports day on the cricket ground. There was also a farmers vs tradesmen cricket match with the men dressed in costume, a concert, dance, bonfire, and of course church services of thanksgiving.

A 'Welcome Home' fund was established for the servicemen and women of Henfield, and by May of that year £100 had been raised. The money was used to provide them with an evening of entertainment and 'momento scrolls' thanking them for services rendered during the war. Two 'welcome home' parties were held in the Assembly Rooms in 1946, and one in 1948 to coincide

102 The High Street decked out with bunting to mark V.E. Day on 8 May 1945. In the bottom left-hand corner can be seen the block house on the corner of Cagefoot Lane by the bus stop.

103 Members of the Henfield Land Army Club in 1947 at 'Furners' in Furners Lane, home of the local representative Miss Gibson, seen here in the middle row, third from left. Holding the toy rabbit is Miss K. Alexander, a pioneer in the Women's Land Army who was awarded a B.E.M. for her work in 1947. The club was in operation from 1939-50.

with service personnel being de-mobilised. Twenty-one young men from Henfield did not return. It was decided by the Parish Council in 1948 that a fitting memorial to those who fell in the Second World War would be to clear, drain and lay out five acres of Henfield Common as playing fields for the village. The work was finally completed in September 1950 with a football pitch and room for two hockey pitches.

As the war came to an end thoughts for future housing needs were being considered by the District Council. Possible sites for future housing were identified at West End Lane and Wantley. In the end Wantley was chosen and work started in October 1946 with the laying of sewers and the construction of a small sewage treatment plant. Initially 12 prefabricated buildings were erected, and they were followed in the next two years by 44 houses now known as 'New Wantley'. The concrete road through the estate was laid by German P.O.W.s.

104 'Welcome Home' party, September 1948. On the extreme right is F. Skilton, and behind him Lucie Bishop, secretary of the organising committee. On the table to the left are Dr H.F. Squire and F. Waite, chairman. In the centre front is John Skilton, and behind and to the right Reg Saunders. Other people in the photograph include Rosie Morris, Bertha Holden, and Bill and Frank Greenfield.

105 The War Memorial on Henfield Common was unveiled by Annette Parsons and Peter Collins. Henfield then played a game of football against Horsham Y.M.C.A. to christen the new pitch.

106 The 'prefabs' at Wantley Hill, built in 1947. These remained until 1965 when they were replaced by six three-bedroomed houses and 20 two-bedroomed flats.

107   Storm damage near Batts Road, October 1987. The 'Great Storm' struck the south of England on the night of Thursday, 15 October 1987. A large number of fallen trees blocked the roads out of the village and brought down power lines. Roads were soon open but it took about ten days to reinstate the electricity supply. Winds and fallen trees caused structural damage to properties but thankfully no one in the village was injured.

The 50th Anniversary of V.E. Day was marked by four days of events during the first week of May 1995. Local traders decorated their shops and the High Street with bunting and union flags and the Museum put on a special exhibition. On 5 May the Henfield and District Lions Club organised a dance in the Village Hall with people dressed in 1940s costume. Over the weekend some 12 street parties were held around the village. Vigils for peace and special church services were also held over the weekend. On the Bank Holiday Monday there was a 'Village Day' on the Common, which included a pig roast and barbecue organised by the B.P. Guild, pony rides, stalls and arena events. This was followed by community singing and a firework display at 9 p.m. On 24 August there was a tea party for all those who participated in the war effort. The 50th anniversary of V.J. Day was marked by a thanksgiving service in St Peter's Church. In 1999 funds were raised to add plaques listing the names of those who fell in both world wars to the war memorial in Cagefoot Lane, and the modified memorial, now surrounded by railings, was dedicated on 9 January 2000.

Six

THE PEOPLE OF HENFIELD

HENFIELD HAS OVER 400 YEARS of practically complete parish registers. The first begins with the marriage of John Woolgar to Elnor Frankwell on 22 May 1595. The first recorded burial was that of Thomas Bartlet on 29 September 1595, and the first recorded baptism was that of Nicholas Gallop on 30 January 1596. Was he the same 'Nocholas Gallope', churchwarden, who signed the Protestation in 1641?

What do these records tell us about the people of Henfield? The later burial records always note the age of the person, but not the cause of death, except rarely when a drowning or other accident is noted. Although Henfield was to escape the 1665 plague that devastated London, it is very sobering to read in the register: 'these people were thought to dye of the plague from 13th September 1609 to 16th January 1610 followinge'. There then follows a list of 61 names from 27 different families. The Smith family lost seven members, the Mercer and Belson families lost six each, and the others, one, two or three each. They were all buried on the south side of the churchyard. Around 1608 the average number of deaths in the parish per year had been 20; for 61 people to die in four months must therefore have had a great effect on the whole village.

The names of some of the families living in Henfield today appear in the register four hundred years ago. The name Holden (already mentioned in 1374) is most frequently mentioned, there being several branches of the family. Other family names frequently mentioned are Belcher, Bridger, Chate, Cooper, Goff, Haine, Jupp, Legg, Mercer, Page, Stenning, Stokes, White and Woolgar. Some common local names appear later, such as Hobbs in 1629, Vinall in 1635, Greenfield in 1685 and Muzzell in 1687.

Other glimpses of the residents of Henfield can be found in various legal documents such as the marriage settlement of Thomas Woolgar, a shoemaker, in 1636 upon his daughter Mary and her husband John Mercer, blacksmith, which included 'twenty roods [5 acres] of land and the tenement' which 'Thomas Woolgar had lately erected and built upon it'. The land had lately been purchased from one 'John Awood, late of Henfield aforesaid tayler'. The land 'abuttinge' (abutted) 'a certain tenement of Peter Goffes towards the north, and the King's highway towards the west, to lands of Thomas

Woolgar towards the east and south'. The 'King's highway' was the High Street and the tenement built by Thomas Woolgar comprised three cottages to the north of the present Congregational church. Both Woolgar and Mercer later signed the 1641 Protestation.

The Woolgar family provide a good example of a long-lived Henfield family, being first mentioned, as we have seen, in the 1374 Custumal, although curiously no Woolgars remain in the village today. By the time of the 1841 census there were 47 members of the family, divided between ten households. There were 48 in 1851, 66 in 1871, and 49 in 1891. A drift away from Henfield began in the 1750s when a Woolgar married a girl from Bramber, had seven sons, and settled there. The coming of the railway made it possible to travel to London and further afield to find work, and many Woolgars settled in Brighton and Hove as the tourist industry developed. The last Woolgar entry in the Henfield church records was the burial of Harry Woolgar on 26 January 1971, aged 90.

108   The tenements mentioned in the 1636 Woolgar deed are shown here next to the Congregational church, *c*.1912.

Thomas Stapleton was born at Stretham Manor in July 1535. His father was a Chichester solicitor who was steward of the Manor of Stretham, responsible for administering the manor for the bishop of Chichester. Thomas Stapleton trained as a priest, but after the Reformation refused to give up his faith, leaving to go abroad, where he joined a seminary for missionary priests at Douai in France and became Professor of Theology. Priests trained there would then return to England to carry on the Catholic faith in secrecy.

In 1660 Henry Bysshopp, who supported the King during the Civil War, was granted the office of the first Post-master-General by King Charles II. In order to prevent complaints about postal delays, he invented the first postmark or 'Bysshopp Mark' showing the date on which a letter was posted. He held this appointment for three years, and then resigned as he was becoming increasingly embittered by the jealousies aroused by his position.

Henry Bysshopp's sister Elizabeth was brought up at Parsonage House when it was owned by their father Thomas Bysshopp. Although the family moved to Parham House when Elizabeth was only eight years old, she must have held fond memories of her childhood at Henfield. She married and became Dame Elizabeth Gresham of Titsey Place, Surrey. In 1661, four years before she died, she purchased from John Woolgar a field on the west side of New Barn Lane, Henfield, now a farm track, but then one of the main north-south roads, and founded the Dame Elizabeth Gresham Charity. The deed of foundation states:

> Upon trust to pay out of the rents and profits of the land, the sum of 10s. 0d. yearly to 'some

109 Thomas Stapleton (1535-98).

110 Portrait of Henry Bysshopp (1606-92). He was born at Parsonage House, but later moved with his family to Parham. When he inherited the family land at Henfield he returned to Parsonage House and remained there until his death.

Godly able minister and preacher of Gods word' whom they shall procure to preach a sermon [in the Parish Church] of Henfield upon 1 Nov., 'usually called Allhallows day' and with the residue to buy as much cloth of the 'piece and worth' of 3s. 6d. a yard, to be cut into parcels, each to contain three yards, and upon 1 Nov. yearly to be given to so many poor people, inhabitants of Henfield, as there [shall be], to make them clothing, but not to sell the same. The sermon not to be preached [by the same] person the following year, nor the people who receive the cloth one year to have any the following year except [there shall not be a] sufficient number of very indigent persons within the parish.

A Gresham Charity conveyance of 1688 introduces us to William Holney of Henfield Place, John Gratwick of Eatons, the only farm in the parish west of the River Adur, Philip Cheale of Shiprods, a considerable estate in 1688, and 'John Norton Yeo' of the farmhouse on the east side of the High Street now known as Norton House. In 1703 the trustees sold timber from the field and with the proceeds purchased for £42 a second field of one and a half acres, known as Pistolowe at the southern end of Grinstead Lane. These two fields are still held by the Gresham Trust today, are still let as pasture, and the proceeds are still spent on clothing for the needy. The practice of giving flannel continued until the Second World War, when with the advent of clothes rationing, a clothing voucher was introduced, to be spent in local shops. Vouchers are still given out at the annual service and distribution of the Dame Elizabeth Gresham awards every 1 November. So, after nearly 340 years, the name of Elizabeth Gresham is still alive in Henfield.

Another trust which benefits the residents of Henfield is the Kindersley Trust. Miss Eleanor Kindersley lived at Kindersley, Upper Station Road. In 1936 she conveyed a bungalow called Hillside in Lower Station Road to a trust. The house was to be let to disabled ex-servicemen or those unable to maintain themselves due to age or infirmity, and they were to pay just one penny in rent, the trust paying all expenses and repairs. It was let in this way for 50 years until 1986, when it was realised that the trust had no funds to repair or maintain the house, so it was sold and the money invested. From the interest received it is now able to give annual grants to a number of village projects or organisations.

William Borrer was born at Potwell, Cagefoot Lane, on 13 June 1781, although his family afterwards moved to Pakyns Manor, Hurstpierpoint. His father was a wealthy corn merchant and land owner, supplying provender for military horses stationed at Brighton, Lewes and other Sussex towns during the Napoleonic Wars. Young William travelled all over Sussex on horseback assisting his father, and in doing so developed an interest in the wild plants that he saw on the way. He returned to Henfield in 1810 upon his marriage to Elizabeth Hall of New Hall, where he lived for a year whilst the home that his father was building for the couple, Barrow Hill House, was finished.

Not very onerous duties in the family business, and an ample income, allowed him plenty of opportunity to devote time to botany, and he rapidly established a remarkable collection of plants in his garden which numbered 6,600 different British species by 1860. He corresponded with the leading botanists of the day, exchanging plants with

111 Upper Station Road, *c.*1914, showing 'Kindersley' on the extreme right, only a few years after it was built.

112 William Borrer, in a photograph of a contemporary watercolour. This painting was taken to Kenya in the mid-20th century by a descendant, and was later destroyed when their farm was burned by the Mau Mau and the family murdered.

113   The east elevation of Barrow Hill House, built for William Borrer in 1811. The main entrance to Barrow Hill House was opposite Springhills on the Shoreham Road. It was a very large house by local standards, and according to the 1841 census had seven household servants. The garden and grounds covered the area now occupied by Mill Drive and Cedar Way.

them. He was elected a fellow of the Linnaean Society in 1805, and was later a fellow of the Royal Society. Many of the monumental botanical taxonomy books of the day contained acknowledgements to his perceptive plant descriptions. It was, however, his work on lichens which was fundamental. He was the first person to realise that lichens will only grow in pure air, an observation which has led to the modern use of lichens for pollution monitoring, and he has often been called 'the father of British lichenology'.

As we have seen, Borrer was also the driving force behind the founding of the three national schools. At one time he presented each boy in the school with a pair of boots and money to have them repaired. He paid for the enlarging of St Peter's Church and, together with Mrs Wood of Chestham Park, also donated £2,000 to increase the vicar's stipend, as at that time the village had suffered from absentee vicars.

Henfield felt a great loss on his death in 1862. The finest plants from his collection, together with his notebooks, correspondence and pressed plants were donated to the Royal Botanic Gardens at Kew. Barrow Hill House was sold in 1863 by his son Dawson Borrer to Eardley N. Hall, William's son-in-law (and cousin). Eardley N. Hall is recorded as having each Christmas presented a barrel of beer to the Boys School. Later Barrow Hill House was occupied by Eardley's son, John Eardley Hall, who lived there with his two sisters. William Borrer's daughter Fanny married the Rev. Charles Dunlop and lived at Red Oaks.

The last descendant of the Borrer family to live at Barrow Hill House was Annette Blackburne-Hall, who died in 1921, after which it remained empty until the war years when troops were billeted there. It was pulled down in the mid-1950s. The rear entrance to the house was from Golden Square past Chatfields, where the coach house and stables have been converted into a house. Although the remarkable garden has now gone, a few rare plants survive on the bank at the top of Barrow Hill, which is now known as 'the Borrer bank'.

Nathaniel Woodard came to Sussex in 1846 as curate in charge of the church and parish of St Mary's, New Shoreham. The following year he opened a small day school close to the gate, and in 1848 a boarding school named St Nicholas after the church at Old Shoreham. This was the beginning of Lancing College, the first of eight schools for boys and eight schools for girls which the Provost and Corporation of St Mary's and St Nicholas now administer. His vision was that the best education should be available to all, and he set out to provide boarding schools for all classes. At that time there were the great public schools for the rich, and national schools for the poor, but only rather

114 The magnificent cedars of Lebanon, seen here lining the left-hand side of the entrance to Springhills, were planted by William Borrer's son Dawson in 1854. There was a storm of protest in 1985 when they were felled in advance of the site being redeveloped. A special public meeting was held in May that year to discuss why this had happened but no amount of talk could bring back the trees.

115   The east elevation of Martyn Lodge, *c.*1870, showing part of its large garden which is now built on. The lady
on the left is Mrs Woodard. In later years an extension was added to this side of the house.

inferior private establishments for the ever-growing middle classes. His first schools were
in Sussex: Lancing College; St John's College, Hurstpierpoint; and St Saviour's, Ardingly.
He planned them to have Christian teaching, each with its own noble and dignified
chapel.

Woodard came to live at Martyn Lodge, Church Street, Henfield in 1862, and it
remained his home until his death in 1891. He was frequently away travelling in the
interests of his schools, supervising the foundation of new ones, and raising the enormous
sums of money needed to build them. He interested some of the leading figures of the
country in contributing to them, and many children from Henfield have enjoyed and
profited by an education at one of the Woodard schools.

The peaceful countryside around Henfield has long made it, like Ditchling, a
retreat for those of an artistic nature. Elizabeth Robins was born in 1862 into a wealthy

family in the southern U.S.A. Against the wishes of her family she became an actress. She first came to London in 1888, and was introduced to the theatre world by Oscar Wilde. In 1908 she introduced the London stage to the works of Henrik Ibsen, and her brilliant performances took London by storm. She began to write novels in 1898, at first under the name C.E. Raimond. Having lost touch with her younger brother, who had departed for the Klondike 'gold rush', she set off to find him. He was seriously ill but she nursed him back to health and later wrote the best-selling book *The Magnetic North* recounting her experiences. She returned to Britain physically weakened, abandoned the stage for writing and, after staying at a friend's cottage to recuperate, decided to purchase a retreat for herself. It was then that she first visited Backsettown, Henfield, and in 1908 it became her Sussex home. Soon afterwards she met Octavia Wilberforce, who joined her there and then decided to become a medical student, not an easy task for a woman at that time.

Backsettown seemed to have such an atmosphere of peace that Robins had the idea of sharing it with those who needed a 'rest pause' in an otherwise stressful life. In November 1927 she opened the 'Backsettown home of rest' for overworked professional women. Many famous people, including Dame Sybil Thorndyke, took advantage of the

116 Backsettown is situated just to the east of Henfield High Street, and was the home of Elizabeth Robins from 1908 until her death in 1952.

opportunity to recuperate in peaceful surroundings. In 1933 Dr Wilberforce was given two Jersey cows, which produced milk and cream for the guests. At the outbreak of the Second World War the land at Backsettown had to be farmed seriously, so Dr Wilberforce formed a herd of Jersey cattle. Being American, Miss Robins had restrictions placed upon her, including having to report to the police, so she reluctantly returned to the U.S.A. Backsettown continued to receive guests and Elizabeth Robins was able to return in May 1945. By now the home had become well known and income had risen, but so had the running costs. On her death in 1952 she bequeathed it to Dr Wilberforce, who continued to run it as a rest home, giving up her medical practice in Brighton.

Octavia Wilberforce was a remarkable woman, showing the same persistence and refusal to be defeated found in her great-grandfather William, the abolitionist M.P. She made a great impression on all those she came into contact with, whether as a doctor, farmer, county councillor, or friend of artists, dramatists and authors. She died on 19 December 1963 and Backsettown continued to be run as a rest home until 1988.

Margaret Fairless Barber was born at Castle Hill, Rastrick, Yorkshire in 1869, the youngest daughter of a lawyer. She trained as a nurse, practising in one of the worst east London slums, the Jago. Ill health dogged her all her life, and nursing proved too strenuous. On the death of her parents she travelled to Germany, and later lived for a time at a roadside lodge in Sussex, where she was visited by her writer friend William Scott Palmer. She was an invalid by this time, and later became seriously ill when she visited him in London. She made a partial recovery, and was adopted into her friend's household, living in a house overlooking the Thames.

She took up writing, using the name Michael Fairless, and produced a number of fragments of prose and poetry, and two longer works, *The Gathering of Brother Hilarius* and *The Grey Brethren*. She returned to Sussex with her friends in the summer of 1900, and stayed at Mockbridge House, north of Henfield. Over the next year or so, in both London and Sussex, she wrote *The Roadmender*, her last and best-known work. She died on 24 August 1901, aged only 32, and was buried at Ashurst churchyard. *The Roadmender*, published in 1902, describes the passing pageant of people seen through the eyes of an old roadmender as he breaks stones for mending holes in the road, and describes the countryside around Mock Bridge, Shermanbury, Henfield and Cowfold. It caught the public imagination and became successful, although the identity of Michael Fairless and the locations mentioned remained a secret until August 1921, the 20th anniversary of Margaret Barber's death. By careful deduction, her identity was revealed, and the 'lean grey downs' identified as the South Downs.

Public interest led to the area being marketed in the 1920s and 1930s as 'roadmender country'. The book went through 45 editions and reprintings in 25 years, and large numbers of visitors came to discover the countryside for themselves, travelling by train and on foot. Although the book is largely forgotten today, the scenery around Mock Bridge, the River Adur with its water meadows, Shermanbury Place, Bottings Farm and

117 Mr and Mrs Frank Bowler at Mockbridge House, *c.*1912, standing outside the room where Margaret Barber wrote *The Roadmender*.

Mockbridge House remain practically unchanged and as peaceful as when they made such an impression on Margaret Barber.

In 1942 Barbara and Dulcima Glasby, stained glass artists, moved to Henfield. Their father, William, had been making stained glass since 1875. After working for a number of well-known artists, he had set up on his own, and received many commissions, including a number for war memorial windows in 1922-3. He supplied stained glass for 100 locations in Britain and 15 overseas, assisted in his later years by Barbara. The largest single commission was a series of 20 windows for the Peachtree Christian Church in Atlanta, Georgia. Eight of these had been completed by 1939, but work had to stop due to the war. William died in 1941, so the remaining 12 windows were completed by both daughters in their studio at Sunnyside, Upper Station Road. This took them eight years, from 1945-53. Following their father's tradition, they established a name for themselves because of their colour rendering. They did their own designing, beginning with a rough sketch and then a complete watercolour miniature of the work, for the client's approval, from which the window would be produced. Dulcima had had

118 Barbara Glasby at work in her studio. In the bottom left are the miniature designs of the window which were first sent to the client for approval. In the background is a full-size 'cartoon' which would be used to produce the final stained glass window.

a previous career in the 1930s writing radio scripts for the B.B.C., and children's stories, but she is best remembered locally for the wool shop she kept in the High Street in the 1960s.

John Gray and his wife Rosa came to live in Henfield in the 1940s. John (1863-1954) produced a large number of pencil drawings and watercolours of the village in the 1940s and would send his friends hand-painted greetings cards. Susan and Hardie (1907-94) Williamson moved to Henfield in 1947 having bought Myrtle Villa in Church Street and converted an old stable in their back garden into a studio. Susan became a fabric designer and Hardie a designer for a large glass manufacturing company in the Midlands. Both had taught art and had had paintings exhibited at the Royal Academy. Hardie was particularly fond of the Lake District, and lakes, rocks and mountains feature in much of his work.

119 The Williamsons in their studio.

120 The studio at 'Dykes'. Both Malcolm and Hilda Milne were keen gardeners and the flowers in their garden gave them plenty of subject matter to paint.

Malcolm Milne (1887-1954) and his sister Hilda came to live at 'Dykes' at the back of Henfield Common in 1926. Both were artists, but the work of Malcolm won national acclaim. He was noted as a painter of flowers, but also painted portraits and landscapes using oils, watercolour and pen and ink. An exhibition of 31 pieces of his work was held in Bond Street, London in 1931, and in 1966, 12 years after his death, a retrospective exhibition of his paintings and drawings was held in the Ashmolean Museum, Oxford. Salford City Art Gallery have examples of his work including a view of Barrow Hill, Henfield. An artist friend of the Milnes was Harold Squire (1881-1959), who came to Henfield in the 1930s and built 'The Hundred' on the Brighton Road.

In 1952 Miss Freda Bond (1894-1973) retired to Henfield with her friend Miss Tann, to live at East Martyns in Church Street. She had been educated at Ipswich High School and Girton College Cambridge, where she had obtained a History degree, and after the First World War went into the civil service. In her spare time she wrote poetry and freelance articles for various magazines and papers. In 1933 she published a novel *The Philanthropist*, and after her retirement concentrated on writing children's books and poetry which led to a literary friendship with John Masefield.

121 Rowland Emett in 1977 with one of his models. He lived in London Road, Henfield in the early 1950s. A cartoonist with *Punch* magazine, he had the opportunity to turn his creations into three dimensions with the 'Oyster Creek and Far Tottering Railway', said to have been inspired by the Henfield railway, at the 1951 Festival of Britain.

Other artistic people who lived in Henfield during the 20th century included the impresario Prince Littler, who lived at Chestham Park; the cartoonist Rowland Emett, who lived at Penny Cottage; the comic writer J.B. Morton ('Beachcomber' of the *Daily Express* newspaper), who lived at Potwell; and for a time in the 1970s the pop singer Adam Faith, who lived at Whaphams.

Up until the mid- to late 20th century there were still a number of family businesses in the High Street which had been in operation for over 50 years. Their owners became household names locally, and even today when they are long gone their names still crop up in general conversation. Longleys started a draper's business in Henfield in 1775. George, the son of the founder, ran the business until his death in 1859, and he was followed by his sons Henry and John. John did not stay in the business long, leaving to become a priest, but Henry carried on until *c.*1903. Their main premises were at Old Bank House and Brick House, High Street. As well as being drapers and tailors, the family were also funeral directors, grocers and furniture dealers at various times. Although not a family business, Hamfelds' hardware shop, the current occupier of Brick House, is now the oldest shop in the High Street, having traded for nearly 50 years.

The Church Street junction with the High Street is still known by many as Cruttenden's corner after the family who ran a baker's shop there for many years. Arthur Cruttenden started his business *c.*1891, and it was taken over by his son Frank in 1932. It was sold in 1965 to A.E. Dunford, but Frank Cruttenden continued to work there part-time until a year before his death in 1983. At one time Cruttenden's had a tea garden, and in common with other traders used to make deliveries, a great rivalry existing between Cruttenden's and Musson's Bakery for customers on their rounds.

The Musson family owned a number of different shops in the High Street over the years. J.T. Musson came to the village *c*.1878 and took over what had been Charles Longley's grocer's shop at the southern end of Bay Tree House. Later the family also acquired Longley's hardware shop, the present Angela's, and in 1931 Henry Moore's baker's shop, now the NatWest Bank. In *c*.1928 the family took over Mr Bowerman's grocer's shop at Brook House which became known as 'top Mussons' because it was at the top of the High Street. It closed in the late 1950s. J.T. Musson was followed by his son John and then by his grandson Vincent before the business left the family. The new owners traded under the name J. Musson and Son Ltd until Holland and Barrett took over their original shop in 1965. It was probably in the early 1900s that the original shop premises were enlarged to their present size.

122 Cruttenden's baker's shop in the 1920s when the doorway was on the corner. From left to right: E. Morey Jnr., E. Morey Snr., H. Hambleton, F. Dowdell, Arthur Cruttenden, Ivy Thompsett and, in the shop, 'Auntie' Burtenshaw.

123 Musson's grocer's shop is shown here on the right in this *c*.1917 view of the High Street. The third shop on the left was their hardware shop and the first on the left was Arthur Hillman's boot shop.

124 The baker's shop of Fred Moore in *c*.1890, which became Musson's bakery in 1931. Left to right: Mr Thompsett, James Scott, Henry Moore and Fred Moore. The Moore family had the business for just under 50 years.

Arthur Hillman, a boot and shoe maker, took over the premises occupied by John Haybittle at Clock House in the High Street in *c*.1900. The business was later carried on by his son Cyril and daughter Nellie until 1983. Another family business spanning more than half a century was that of J.F. Bowden & Son, tailors and outfitters in Church Street. The business was started by John Bowden in 1906 and on his retirement around the time of the Second World War his son Mervyn took over. This was where school-children were fitted with their uniforms. The business closed in 1965 but the family name lives on in the house name.

The Thorns family of farmers and butchers had a shop in Jasmine House for over 100 years. John Thorns who took over the shop from Elizabeth Pattenden in *c*.1845 was followed by his sons John and Thomas and then his grandson Frank from *c*.1889-1938 and finally by his great grandson Nelson until the 1950s. London House in the High Street had always been a watch and clock maker's shop. Douglas Funnell took over the premises from John Alliss in 1933, and was followed by his son Robin who carried on the business until 1987. The family used to wind the clocks in both the Assembly Rooms and St Peter's Church.

125   Thorns butcher's shop, *c*.1920. Frank Thorns is on the left and Archie Buckett is on the right. The passage up the side of the shop led to the butcher's croft.

126 Douglas and Robin Funnell working in their shop in London House in 1965. Even after retirement in 1987 Robin Funnell continued to repair clocks and watches for old customers.

The Tobitt family were in business in Henfield for nearly 100 years. Samuel Tobitt came to Henfield in *c.*1856 and took over a small draper's and grocer's shop which had been run by Messrs Baldwin & Garrett on the site of the present-day Budgens. Samuel was followed in the business by his sons Charles and 'Fred'. Charles would sit at his desk in the window running the business, whilst his brother stayed in the background looking after the accounts. The shop was very Dickensian, having one outside toilet and no water supply, and it continued to use gas lamps long after electricity came to the village. The business expanded to include furniture and antiques, which were sold from Elm Lodge and Brick House. Charles Tobitt became a wealthy man, having bought much property in Henfield and Hove. On his death in 1953 the business was sold. 'Fred' died in 1957, and his sister Ada, the last family member living in Henfield, died at Rus House in 1969 aged 96. All the family were musical; Charles played the organ at the Congregational church and also the violin, which could often be heard in his room above the shop.

The Morris family of boot and shoe makers came to Henfield from Cowfold in the 1820s. Originally there were two brothers, Charles and George, who acquired two shops in the High Street. Charles was followed by his son Thomas through to the 1860s, and George by his son Daniel, and then his grandsons who traded under the name of Morris Bros through to the late 1920s.

A couple still remembered by many people in the village were Charles Tyler and his wife Mary. They came to Henfield after their marriage in Brighton in 1890 and opened a hairdresser's and sweet shop. In 1894 they moved premises to what is now Village Care. Charles Tyler cut hair at the back of the shop, often whistling hymns as he did so, whilst Mary ran what was described as a 'fancy repository' at the front of the

127 The High Street, looking north in 1950. On the right is Samuel Tobitt's draper's and grocer's shop, and next to that what used to be Morris Bros. boot and shoe shop. These buildings were all demolished in the 1980s and replaced by the modern Budgens, a pastiche of the original.

128 Charles Tobitt at the organ in the Congregational church.

129 Mr and Mrs C. Tyler outside their shop in 1949. Mr Tyler was an ardent campanologist and helped with the formation of the Sussex County Association of Change Ringers. He gave unbroken service as a bell ringer at St Peter's Church for nearly 50 years.

130   St Peter's handbell ringers, *c.*1896. Left to right: Lazarus Payne, William Hillman, George Payne, Henry Stringer (standing), Charles Tyler, John Alliss, Alfred Groves.

shop. Anything could be bought there, from needles and cotton to toys and patent medicines. Charles was cutting hair up until the time of his death in December 1950 at the age of 89 years. Mary ran the shop alone for a short period and then retired, dying in 1955 aged 91 years.

Rolf Ruff was in business in Henfield as a cycle teacher and dealer *c.*1902, when he had premises at the bottom of the High Street. In *c.*1904, when Commercial Buildings were built, he moved into what is now the northern part of Wine Rack. There was a workshop at the back where he repaired bicycles, and instructions on how to ride were given on Henfield Common. His son Fred carried the business on through to the early 1960s when he retired with his wife to New Zealand. The cycle business was carried on by J.T. Wilkins until *c.*1967.

131   Commercial Buildings, *c*.1906. On the left was the shop of Percy Brooks, the colonial butcher, then that of Rolf Ruff. Next were the Grimsby Fish Stores and Pattenden's newsagents and fancy goods shop. The fish shop did not last long, and by 1908 Thomas Baines the draper was occupying the premises.

Frank Norman 'Nobby' Clarke was a senior partner in a Brighton accountancy firm and lived in Henfield for about 25 years. At the time of his death in 1945 he was Chairman of Henfield Parish Council, and Assistant District Commissioner for the Scouts. He was a great benefactor to the scouts and was involved in many other organisations including the Nursing Division of the St John Ambulance, the Henfield and District Ambulance Club and the fire brigade.

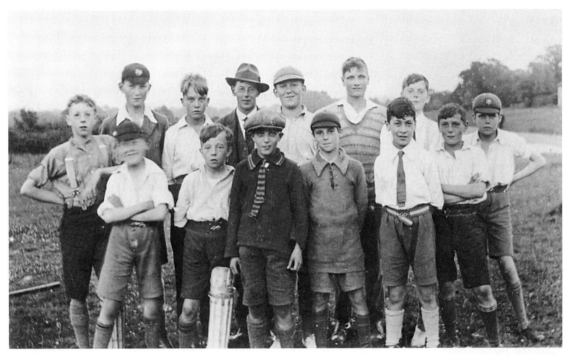

132   Ron Shepherd always wore a trilby hat, and is seen here with a group of boys on Henfield Common *c*.1930. Percy Groves to his left and Arthur Parsons in the middle of the front row would both later play cricket for Henfield.

133 & 134   The Tanyard pond and buildings in the 1940s. Note the traditional hay ricks. Bill Goacher used this land from the 1940s until his death. Bill Goacher (inset) next to the Tanyard pond in 1965.

135 In 1963 when this photograph was taken Henfield was much smaller and people knew their postman. Most of them came from long established families. From left to right: Henry Holder, Frank Skilton, Den Fowler, Noel Furnival, Stan Carey, John Barwick, Tom Thorns, Len Crook.

Ron Shepherd (1903-77) was born in Henfield and lived in the village all his life. He never married, devoting his life to St Peter's Church and to the youth of the village. He sang in the choir, acted as a server, and for 50 years trained others to follow on with these duties. As well as forming a number of sports clubs, he organised the A.R.P. messenger boys during the Second World War, and was instrumental in starting the Air Training Corps in Henfield.

Bill Goacher, who died in 1981, was one of Henfield's old characters. He would usually be seen cycling round the village wearing his hat and brown knee-length coat, with his collie dog in tow. He spoke in a strong Sussex dialect which was recorded for the B.B.C. archives. He was involved with farming all his life, having been brought up at 'Frogshole', West End Lane. He later managed Rye Farm for Charles Tobitt, but will be remembered by many for his long association with the Tanyard Field. Here he kept chickens and ducks and a few other animals. He planted crocuses around the 'Coronation Oak' on Pinchnose Green, which serve as his living memorial.

Seven

HENFIELD AT LEISURE

A SURVEY CARRIED OUT IN 1947 showed there were 28 clubs and associations in the village; today that number is around sixty-two. Some of the clubs have come and gone, whilst others are still going after more than 100 years. Of the ten sports clubs, that with the longest history is the cricket club. The game is recorded as having been played at Henfield in 1721, and a 'Henfield' team played at Hurstpierpoint in 1719, although during this time the Henfield team was not properly established, and groups of men, usually from the upper classes, would play each other, often for a wager. A team might call itself Henfield, but may have been made up of players from outside the county.

By 1771 a more established team was playing, and by the early 19th century there was a growing feeling that the Henfield team should be made up solely of men from the locality, which led in May 1837 to the formation of Henfield Cricket Club, properly constituted with rules and regulations. In the 19th century the club featured prominently amongst the clubs of Sussex. Thirty-three of Henfield's players played for the county side between 1823 and 1905, including three captains.

The popularity of the local game went into a steady decline from the 1880s through to the early 1900s but the club fortunes were revived by the new vicar, the Rev. R.J. Lea, when he came to the village in 1913. He brought the game to the public eye, with articles in the parish magazine, and suggested that a cricket match should form part of the peace celebrations in 1919. After the First World War, thanks to Lea and J.F. Stephenson, cricket was again being played regularly on the Common. In 1926 money was raised to build a pavilion, opened by A.E.R. Gilligan, captain of England, on 13 July that year. During the 1920s the playing area was also extended and fenced. Generations of the same families have played cricket for Henfield. J. Thorns played for Henfield in 1838, for example, and his descendants still play for the club today. At the present time the club has first and second teams in the Sussex Invitation League, and also plays friendly matches, whilst three 'colts' teams cater for players under 14 years of age.

The other main sporting activity has been football. Henfield Football Club was formed in 1889, and originally played in a red strip. Early games were played on *The*

136 Married versus singles cricket match, *c.*1912. Standing fourth from left is P. Brooks, seventh from left is W. Purkis, 10th F. Dewdney, 12th C. Tyler, and 13th W. Pattenden.

George field. In 1919-20 they became 'Henfield Athletic Football Club', and entered a team in the Horsham League for the first time. After the First World War the club played on a field on the corner of the entrance to Backsettown, before transferring to a field at Wantley Hill. They used both the Eardley Hall Institute and *The George Hotel* as a club headquarters before the Second World War. After the building of the Wantley Hill estate, they moved to 'Nobby' Clark's field in Furners Lane, where they had a wooden hut which served as a changing room. Prior to this, home team players would arrive kitted up ready to play, whilst away players would change in *The Bell Inn*. At this time the club had three teams, the third team usually playing on the Daisy Croft. When the War Memorial football pitch was formed on the Common in 1950, all games were played there.

In *c.*1921 Ron Shepherd started the St Peter's Junior Cricket and Football Clubs, which were open to boys aged 9-15 years. For the 1921-2 season the Boys School entered a team in the South Downs Elementary Schools Football League, and it is believed they played on a field behind *The Plough Inn*. In 1956 Ron's club had the use of the Daisy Croft as a football pitch, and fielded two teams. A small hut on the site doubled as a changing room and a place where the club's non-competitive section could meet. In the 1930s Shepherd also formed a team of tradesmen who played on Wednesdays on the field at Wantley Hill. In the 1930s and 1940s the Backhouse Poultry Farm had a team which played friendly matches on a field in Kidders Lane, about a mile north of the village. The Henfield Working Men's Club formed a sporting section in 1913, and they also played football on *The George* field until about the time of the First World War. A women's team was also formed after the Second World War, and in the 1950s played on the Daisy Croft. In 1973 a Sunday men's club was formed, called the

137   Henfield Athletic Football Club, 1956-7, Horsham Charity Cup winners. Standing, left to right: E. Colgate, J. Short, F. Skilton, B. Woolven (Pat Collins on his shoulders), R. Wales, R. Skilton, J. Pollard, G. Golds. Kneeling: Peter Collins, J. Lewry, A. Robertson.

'Henfield Mohawks', and in 1990 a youth club girls' team was formed. In 1993 Henfield Athletic Football Club joined with Henfield Mohawks, Henfield Boys Sports Club and Henfield Youth Club girls' team to form the Henfield Football Club. The club now has six pitches at its disposal, three at the leisure centre, two on the Henfield Common, and one on the Rothery Field.

Little is known about the history of the Henfield quoits club, except that the game was being played from *c*.1900 through to the 1920s, and possibly into the 1930s. The players used a quoit weighing 6 lb. and threw it 18 yards to a pin, or 'hob' as it was called, set into the ground. Two points were awarded if the quoit encircled the 'hob', with one point for each quoit closer to the 'hob' than the opponent's. The first team to reach 21 points would win.

Other games that have been played on the Common include ladies hockey and stoolball. The Ladies Hockey Club was formed in December 1920, and probably played on the cricket pitch. In the early 1930s mixed hockey was being played on a sloping field at Staples Barn, the barn itself being used as a place to serve teas and buns after the game. When the Memorial Playing Fields were created, they included room for two hockey pitches. In 1955 a meeting was held at Potwell in Cagefoot Lane and the

138 Quoits were played on the triangular piece of grass in front of the Violet Nurseries at the western end of Henfield Common. The wooden covers protected the pins and the soft ground around them.

139   Boys and girls playing stoolball on the Tanyard field, *c.*1910, with C. Collis, Headmaster of the Boys School, acting as umpire. Games were more usually played in the Kings Field or on Henfield Common.

Henfield Ladies Hockey Club was formed with Mrs Jean Freeman as its first president. Matches were played on the Common, and teas taken in the sun room at Potwell. Matches were played against teams from all over Sussex, and the club also entered tournaments outside the county. A few mixed matches were also played. By the late 1970s membership numbers had declined, and the club closed in the 1980s.

Stoolball is an old Sussex game which is known to have been played at Henfield from the Edwardian period onwards, but early records of the club have been lost. In 1924 Miss W. Peters was secretary and matches were being played on the cricket pitch, which became the regular venue. From the end of the Second World War through to 1978, when the club disbanded, the team played friendly, league, and inter-county matches and, over the years, several of the players were picked to play for Sussex. Stoolball is still played in the neighbouring village of Blackstone.

The larger houses in the village had their own lawn tennis courts, and the game was played as a part of the social scene by the middle and upper classes. A Henfield Tennis Club was in existence in the 1890s, and probably played on two grass courts belonging to Henfield Place in what is now the King's Field, but must have disbanded, because in the 1920s the Rev. Lea called a meeting at the Eardley Hall Institute, and from this a small club was formed. The first games were played on a field in Sandy Lane after it had been cut for hay, and later games were played on the west side of

140   Two games of tennis in progress on the Kings Field, *c*.1912.

London Road opposite Wantley Manor. Leading up to the Second World War three courts were used on the site of Greenways, at the northern end of Broomfield Road, whilst during the war tennis was played on a hard court at Martyn Lodge. After the war the courts at Greenways were not resurrected, and in April 1947 the club tried to obtain permission to use part of the King's Field. The proposal was initially rejected by the Parish Council, but was later approved and in October 1951 two grass courts were laid at the northern end of the field. At this time the club also had the use of a hard court at Broomfields, the home of Dr H.F. Squire. In 1953 a hut was erected at the King's Field as a changing room and store, then replaced by a larger pavilion in the late 1950s which had once been a summer house belonging to Miss Bowler. The club gained its first hard court in 1962 with the aid of a loan from the Sussex County Playing Fields Association. In 1967 a second hard court was laid, and a third in 1979. Planning permission for a new pavilion was obtained in 1969 and it was completed in 1971. The club joined the Lawn Tennis Association in 1972, and began playing league tennis for the first time. Today the club is very active, with a membership of 200 including 80 juniors.

Badminton started to be played in the Assembly Rooms from the late 1920s, but when a permanent stage was provided the court became too small for league games so only friendly matches could be played. Once the new Village Hall was opened in 1974 league and friendly matches were played there. When the Sports Centre opened in 1990, a second club called the Henfield and District Badminton Club was formed.

The Henfield Bowling Club was formed in 1929 and played at Golden Square. There were three rinks, but the game could only effectively be played away from the road, as there was nothing to stop the woods hitting the wall and iron railings at the road side. Equipment was kept in a small wooden hut at the back of the green. This was too small to act as a pavilion so refreshments were taken at the Comrades Club at the top of the High Street. Mr Baigent, who owned the land, gave it to the club shortly before his death in 1958. By the late 1960s the club was looking for a better site and was exploring the possibility of playing on the Kings Field, or on Henfield Common. In 1972 they obtained planning permission for a new green with six rinks and a pavilion on land to the east of Furners Mead. The green was opened on 1 June 1974 with a match against the Sussex C.B.A. Executive team. The club is now fully integrated and has 63 men and 45 women members, some of whom are county players, who play in three leagues as well as cup and friendly matches.

The introduction of the August Bank Holiday in 1884 marked the start of an annual sports day held on the Common, which continued until the 1920s. This was open to people of all ages in Henfield and surrounding villages. In 1905 there were 27 events which included egg and spoon races, slow bicycle race, human wheelbarrow race, hopping race, three legged race, sack race, 50 yd. and 100 yd. sprint, steeplechase and tug-of-war.

141 The bowling green at Golden Square in 1935 in the foreground. The sale of this land for development as flats funded the new bowling green to be provided in 1974.

142   An August Bank Holiday pram race was a regular fund-raising event for local good causes from the 1960s
through to the early 1980s. Men dressed up as mother and child would run the 1½ miles around the village
consuming half a pint of beer each in the pubs on the way. The winning team's pub would stage the event the
following year, so the starting point varied. In this photograph taken in 1964 the start was in Cagefoot Lane.

The first flower show to be held in Sussex was on Henfield Common in 1856,
initiated by William Borrer. Just over 100 years later, on 11 March 1957, the Henfield
Flower Club was formed. The club originally met at *The George Hotel* but now meets in
the Henfield Hall. Formed in 1884, the Henfield and District Chrysanthemum Society
is still in existence today, making it the oldest society in the village, and it now calls
itself the Chrysanthemum, Dahlia and Horticultural Society. After the war the Village
Produce Association concentrated on growing vegetables, and in 1948 a weekly produce
stall was set up on the corner of Cagefoot Lane. This stall was initially kept on the
ground opposite the blacksmiths and later at Potwell, and had to be moved backwards
and forwards from there. The Village Produce Association remains very active today.

The idea of forming a scouting movement for boys came about following discus-
sions which took place between Lord Robert Baden-Powell and Major A.G. Wade on
their way home from South Africa after the Boer War. Major Wade had been born in
Henfield, and his father was C.A. Wade, solicitor of Croft House. In August 1907, as is
well documented, Baden-Powell held the first scout camp on Brownsea Island, Dorset.
It is believed that in the autumn of that year, Miss Audrey Wade, Major Wade's sister,

started a scout troop in Henfield from members of the boys' hockey club. Miss Wade was assisted by Miss Sybil Mead, and Major Wade, who, as well as starting a troop at Chichester, also became instructor of the Henfield troop.

The first headquarters for the scouts was a barn at Hacketts, close to the cemetery, and in 1917 they moved to what is now the Henfield Club in Cagefoot Lane. The Rev. A.L. Panchard relaunched the scouts in 1917, operations of the troop having been badly affected in the early war years. In 1919 the scout troop and cub pack was officially registered by the second scout master Thomas Clarkson, who had moved to Henfield in 1918 to become headmaster of the Boys School. With the formation of the Comrades

143 The Village Produce Association stall on the corner of Cagefoot Lane was a feature of Saturday morning life from 1948 until the late 1970s when it closed due to complaints from local residents. The W.I., who had been involved with the stall, continued to sell produce in the Village Hall and later in an upstairs room in *The George Hotel* until the mid-1980s.

144 Members of the Girls' Friendly Society putting on a 'pageant of the months' in the garden of Henfield Place in 1934. From left to right: J. Vigars, C. Backshaw, F. Tourle, O. Moss, M. Evans, J. Lewry, E. Linfield, J. Coles, I. Dalmon, E. Aukett, B. Fry, M. Woolgar. The Henfield Branch was formed in 1877, and catered for girls of seven years of age and upwards. A driving force in the organisation was Miss Knowles who was president for many years. On her death in 1947 she left £700 to the society, which continued to operate through to the early 1960s.

145 A gathering in the scouts' field in 1952. In the back-ground is the old army hut which gave good service until the present hut was opened in 1971 by one of Henfield's original scouts, Harold Mitchell.

Club after the war, the scouts had to vacate their headquarters. An old army hut was purchased, and the scouts moved to their new headquarters on the present scouts' field to the west of the High Street in September 1920. The field was originally owned by the Wade family, but was later bought by Frank N. Clarke, who presented the scouts with the freehold of the site in 1933. There have been many scout masters and cub masters over the years, with women playing an important role before the Second World War. The scout movement continues to thrive in Henfield today, with beaver and cub packs, a scout troop and venture unit, catering for boys from the ages of six to 20 years.

On 15 November 1917 Olave, Lady Baden-Powell spoke at a meeting held in Henfield, which led to the formation of a guide movement in the village that December. Miss Ethel Dixon-Brown became Captain of the 1st Henfield Guides, and her sister Hilda ran the rosebuds, later to become the brownies. The first meetings were held in the conservatory at their home, Martyn Lodge. When the founder left the village in 1919 Miss Kaye and Miss Lewis took over control of the guides and brownies. During 1921 a ranger company was formed with Miss Lewis as the captain and Miss E. Baines

146   In November 1958 a group of eight former scouts came together to form the Henfield branch of the Baden-Powell Guild. By the end of the first year membership had increased to forty-three. Members are seen here at camp in 1981. The guild raises around £7,000 annually for the scouts, guides and other organisations.

147 Brownies in the garden of Martyn Lodge with Hilda Dixon-Brown, *c.*1928. Standing, from left to right: Hilda Asher, unknown, Dorothy Franks, Amy Groves, Norah Trower. Kneeling, left: Rose Wilding. Sitting: Margaret Brazier, Vera Tyrell, unknown.

as the assistant. In the early 1920s the Dixon-Browns returned to Henfield. They made a building adjacent to Tannery Cottage available to the guides as a headquarters and furnished it, and it was officially opened in December 1924. Today the building is a private residence called Tannery Barn. A lack of leadership during the late 1920s forced the guides and brownies to close in 1929.

In 1940 Miss Tattershall of Henfield Girls School restarted the company with six evacuees from London, and in 1942 membership of the company was extended to include local girls. Members of the Women's Land Army Club took over the leadership in 1941, a ranger unit had been reformed by 1945, and meetings were now being held in the millhouse granary on the Common.

Guiding continued to flourish in the post-war years under the leadership of Connie Browning and Peggy Whiting, whilst Connie Jupp restarted the brownies in 1950. As time went on more guide, brownie and ranger units were started, and a younger group, the rainbows, was formed. The guides had been sharing the scout hut, so by the 1970s the movement needed a home of its own. Two obsolete sectional classrooms were purchased from a school in Crawley, and under persuasion from Ann Collins the B.P. Guild worked for two years converting them into one large hall with kitchen and toilet facilities, all the money for the project having been raised locally. The guide hut at Staples Barn was officially opened by Grace Stringer, one of Henfield's earliest guides, in October 1982.

The Henfield Trefoil Guild, part of the Sussex Central Trefoil Guild, was formed in March 1979 by Peggy Jenkins, Kath Cruttenden and other former guides. The guild now has 27 members and provides support to the local guides and brownies by helping with various activities and badge work. The guild met at Potwell until 1988, and now hold their monthly meetings at Sobell Court.

148 In 1944 the Henfield Young Farmers' Club was formed. This was open to young people aged 11-25 years, and they met at *The George Hotel*. It organised an annual gymkhana and dog show, social events, farm visits and held talks, but seems to have died out in the late 1960s. Members are seen here in 1948 with their banner, which was presented to them by Lady Davidson. The joint leaders were local farmers Mr Banks and Mr Browning, and Benson Coleman was Chairman.

The first youth club in the village was formed in February 1946. Its aim was to 'further the spiritual, educational, physical and general welfare of its members', and it was open to young people aged from 14 to 21 years. Initially its members came from the Girls Training Corps and the Air Training Corps. The club seems to have continued through until the 1950s, and then a new youth club was formed in January 1959. This started with a membership of 30, catering for those aged between nine and 18 years. The club house was and is the old Infants School in Nep Town Road. In 1960 the club took control of this building, and over the years has enlarged the facilities there, being administered and managed by trustees and a management committee. The St Peter's Youth Club was formed in 1964 from the St Peter's Guild juniors and, like the Henfield Youth Club, is still in existence today.

The building of the Assembly Rooms in 1885 gave the village a place where theatrical and musical societies could perform. The Henfield Choral Society was formed in 1886 and seems to have started and stopped a number of times during its early history. In the early 1950s it was revived by the Rev. P.M. Barry with the aim of

149 The 'Imps' won first prize in the 1937 Coronation Carnival with the 'Rocket', seen here at Golden Square.

studying and performing choral works. During the 1960s the society started to stage operettas and comic operas, in particular those of Gilbert and Sullivan, and this brought about a change of name in 1966 to the 'Henfield Choral and Operatic Society'.

The Henfield Players were formed in 1929 out of what had been the Henfield Arts Club. Many performances have been staged over the years in the Assembly Rooms, and later in the Village Hall. There have been some memorable productions over the years such as *Miranda* in 1959, *Tom Jones* in 1979, *Terra Nova* in 1984, and their 100th production took place in 1976 with *The Madwoman of Chaillot*. In 1999 they combined with the Choral and Operatic Society to become the Henfield Theatre Company. Bertha Holden had a long association with the Henfield Players. At the age of 17, in 1929, she played the part of an aged drunken cook in *Lord Richard in the Pantry*, and her last performance in 1993 aged 81 was as Granny Trill in *Cider with Rosie*. Over the years she also produced some 36 productions. Another operatic group starting in the 1930s, of which Bertha Holden was a member, was 'The Imps'. This was made up from members from the 'Junior Imperial League', a branch of which had been formed by Miss Knowles

and Miss Standen in 1928. They performed operettas and staged variety shows through to the end of the Second World War.

The Henfield and District Angling Society was probably formed in the 1920s and used *The George Hotel* as its headquarters. The membership is currently about 200, and they now meet in the Henfield Club. The club has fishing rights on the Adur from Stretham Bridge to Mock Bridge, as well as parts of the Chess Brook, Batts Pond, fishing lakes at Kirdford, and a pond at Hurstpierpoint. The other angling club in the village is the Comrades Angling Club. This was an offshoot of the Comrades Club and

150   The Henfield Angling Society competition team in the 1930s. Back row, left to right: T. Sawyer, G. Pierce, F. Durrant, W. Cherriman, F. Humphrey, C. Gillett, E. Watts, E. Brown. Front row: B. Fish, A. Knight, T. Page, N.K. Newman, W.T. Waugh, A.J. Standing, C. Fish.

151 The 'Rainbow Temperance Hotel and Coffee House' (now Woodward's, butchers), *c*.1910, when Mr W.G. Purkis was the caretaker. In *c*.1914 the upstairs room was extended outwards so that two billiards tables could be accommodated.

was originally formed in 1946 for ex-servicemen. Today it has a membership of about 50, and has fishing rights on the Adur from the fork where the East and West Adur meet northwards to West Grinstead.

To combat the perceived evils of the public house there were temperance clubs, such as the Henfield Provident Club established in 1842 by the Rev. Charles Dunlop. By 1919 the membership of the club had dwindled and they were drawing on their reserve funds and no doubt closed soon afterwards. The 'Rainbow Temperance Hotel and Coffee House' in the High Street was built in 1880, and also served as the headquarters of the Henfield Cycling Club, cycling being a very popular pastime in the late Victorian and Edwardian periods. In 1901 the Henfield Working Men's Club was formed and rented two rooms in the coffee tavern for £5 8s. 6d. per annum. There was a 15-strong committee and the first president was John Eardley Hall, owner of the property. The club only opened during the winter months and its main activities were whist drives. In 1906 a new club was formed but it called itself by its old name.

Mr Hall died in 1915, and to mark his memory the club and premises became the Eardley Hall Memorial Institute in 1920. This was mainly a social club where young working men could play billiards, etc., and had a library run by Miss Edith Tucker. It closed during the war years and opened again in February 1945, but by the late 1940s membership numbers were declining. Things did not improve through the 1950s, so it closed in 1962. Closure of the club may have been due in part to the 'Comrades of the Great War Club' just a few yards away, which offered similar facilities. This club opened on the corner of Cagefoot Lane on 11 November 1920, and became the local head-quarters of the British Legion in 1921. The British Legion absorbed many ex-servicemen's clubs, but the name 'Comrades Club' was retained until 1975 when it became the Henfield Club. In 1995, due to a lack of members, the Henfield British Legion branch closed and was absorbed into the Cowfold and District Branch. A change of name to the Sussex Weald Branch took place in 2000. A women's branch was formed at Henfield in 1971 and is still active today.

Henfield decided to form a branch of the Women's Institute, when Mrs Watts, who had started the movement in Canada, came to speak in the Assembly Rooms on 17 October 1917. She spoke of her monthly social gatherings of women in rural Canada which brought women of all ranks together for the good of their homes and their community. The first meeting in Henfield was held on 26 October of that year in the Rainbow coffee tavern. Miss Robins of Backsettown was in the chair. Fifty-nine women joined that evening, and other names were added later. Henfield was the second W.I. to be formed in Sussex, Singleton having been the first. In May 1920 the kitchen of the Assembly Rooms was taken over as the W.I. room.

There were monthly meetings with lectures, demonstrations and small internal competitions, new skills were learned and outings were organised. An active dramatic group produced plays and pageants, and there was a W.I. choir. The National Federation of Women's Institutes also organised county, regional and national competitions in cookery, embroidery, choral singing, and the making of scrapbooks to record village history. They produced elaborate dramatic and choral performances such as the *Brilliant and the Dark*, held at the Royal Albert Hall, in which Henfield members took part. Members entered enthusiastically into competitions, often winning high awards. In 1930 the W.I. staged the first Henfield Summer Show, which took a whole year to organise and raise enough money for the hire of a large marquee. Except during the war years, this show was held annually, usually in the gardens of one of the larger houses in the village, until 1967, when it was first held on Henfield Common. Shows continued to be staged mainly on the common until 1983, after which the Junior Mixed School closed, and its facilities were lost. The show then moved to the Village Hall for two further

152 The Henfield W.I. presented the seat in the High Street outside Croft House to the village in February 1954 to celebrate the coronation of Queen Elizabeth II the previous year. Standing, left to right: Mrs Moore, Miss Sylvester-Evans, Mrs Scott, Miss Miles, unknown, Mrs Sayers, Mrs Hammond, Mrs Allston, Mrs Kerslake, Mrs Hubner, May Morey (president), Mrs Leach, Miss Piper. Seated: Mrs Watson, Mrs Martin, Lucie Bishop (secretary), Mrs Baxter.

seasons, but it had lost the atmosphere of a village show and ended with the 50th show in 1985.

In April 1957 a second W.I. group was formed, which met in the evenings for those who were unable to attend afternoon meetings. It was named Tipnoak W.I. after the medieval name for the Henfield Hundred, and the first President was Barbara, Lady Oliver. The two W.I. groups joined forces to run the summer shows and Christmas carol evenings, and had a combined W.I. Choir. In 1964 the two Henfield W.I.s won the Denman Cup, with higher marks at the Dairy Show at Olympia than the rest of the country. All the ingredients were 'wild' and 'free', ranging from pigeon egg meringues, wild cherry soup and smoked eel to hare and rabbit pie. The Tipnoak W.I. closed in 1994.

153 A Darby and Joan Club was started in the village in 1952 under the auspices of the W.V.S. The club started with a membership of 50 and was run by Mrs D. Ransom and Mrs I. Whittome. Members are seen here in the Parish Room in the 1950s, celebrating the wedding anniversary of Mr and Mrs A. Brown, Standing on the right is Nurse Wooller. In 1985 the name was changed to the Good Companions Club.

Perhaps ironically, in view of their pagan origins, May Day revels were re-introduced in the village by the Rev. W. Wakeford when he became vicar in 1899, and were continued by his successor the Rev. Lea. In 1902 the May Queen was Mabel Dewdney, selected by her fellow members of the Band of Hope. The procession formed on Henfield Common, where the May Queen lived, and with her mounted on a small white horse and attended by nine maids of honour and nine page boys the procession, accompanied by some 200 children, proceeded to the church. After a short service, it wended its way back to the common where the May Queen was crowned. This was followed by singing and dancing around the maypole. The last May Day celebrations in the village were probably in 1934 at the vicarage, but the schools continued to have maypole dancing after the war.

154 Annual church fêtes have long been established in the village. The picture shows the church fête in the vicarage garden in 1936 with the Rev. R.J. Lea on the platform.

155 A May Day event taking place outside the White House on Henfield Common in the 1920s. Early May Day events were usually held at the vicarage, but sometimes on Henfield Common or Windmill Hill at Nep Town.

156 A carnival float in 1919 in Vinalls Yard in Nep Town Road, depicting 'the old woman who lived in a shoe'. The 'old woman' is Nurse Wooller. Holding the horse is Albert Brown.

157 All the royal coronations and jubilees have been celebrated in the village. Here we see the 1953 coronation carnival procession passing through the High Street on the way to Henfield Common having paraded around the village.

Other annual events were Empire Day celebrations on Henfield Common, which included the singing of patriotic songs, and the village carnival. A carnival procession would parade around the village and end up at *The George* field or Henfield Common, where prizes were awarded for the best floats, etc. The last annual carnival took place in the late 1940s or early 1950s.

By 2001 Henfield had grown to the size of a small town, with a population of just over 5,000. However it still retains the atmosphere of a village, due in no small part to the many long established families and the various clubs, societies and other organisations which bind the community together.

Bibliography

Copies of items marked* are available for study to *bona fide* researchers by appointment in Henfield Museum.

General

*Armstrong, J.R., *A History of Sussex*, 4th edn., (Phillimore, Chichester, 1995)

*Bishop, L. (ed.), *Henfield in the News*—newspaper cuttings etc. collected by Alice Standen and Lucie Bishop (Henfield, 1938)

*Bishop, L., *Henfield Remembered* (Lucie Bishop, Henfield, *c*.1970)

*Census Returns for Henfield, 1841-1891

*De Candole, H., *The Story of Henfield* (Combridges, Hove, 1947)

*Henfield Ratepayers and Residents Association (1980-92) Review [newsletter]

Leslie, K. and Short, B. (eds.), *An Historical Atlas of Sussex* (Phillimore, Chichester, 1999)

*Morey, M., *I Remember* (May Morey, Henfield, *c*.1999)

*St Peter's Parish Church, Henfield (1902-2000) Parish Magazines

St Peter's Parish Church, Henfield, Parish Registers

*St Peter's Parish Church, Church Rate Accounts 1830-1841

Trevelyan, G.M., *English Social History* (Longmans, London, 1942)

Chapter One, Henfield's Origins

*Barker, E., 'Charter of Osmund, King of the West Saxons, granted in 770 A.D. to Earl Warbald to assign land for the endowment of a church at Henfield'. *Sussex Archaeological Collections*, vol. 86 (1947)

Brighton Archaeological Society, *Excavation of the Stretham moated site* (in press)

Campbell, J., *The Anglo-Saxon State* (Hambledon & London, London, 2000)

Curwen, E.C., *The Archaeology of Sussex* (Methuen, London, 1937)

Hoskins, W.G., *The Making of the English landscape* (Hodder & Stoughton, London, 1955)

*Hudson, T.P. (ed.), *The Victoria County History of the Counties of England. Sussex, Volume VI, Part 3. Bramber Rape (North-Eastern Part).* (Oxford University Press, 1988)

*Johnson, C., *Report and post excavation assessment on the archaeological evaluation (stages 1 & 2) at Furners Lane, Henfield, West Sussex*, Project 1117 (Archaeology South East, Ditchling, Sussex, 1999)

Margary, I.D., *Roman Ways in the Weald* (Phoenix House, 1948)

Morris, J. (ed.), *Domesday Book: Vol. II, Sussex* (Phillimore, Chichester, 1985)
*Peckham, W.D., 'Sussex Custumals: Custumal of Bishop William Rede, 1374'. *Sussex Record Society 31*, 104-125
Rackham, O., *The History of the Countryside* (Dent, London, 1986)
West Sussex County Planning Department: Archaeological Sites and Monuments Record

Chapter Two, Communications
Barnes, P., *The Steyning Line Rail Tour* (Philip Barnes, 2001)
Campbell, A.C., *The Baybridge Canal to West Grinstead* (1976)
Dale, A., *Brighton Town and Brighton People* (Phillimore, Chichester, 1976)
Gray, A., *The Railways of Mid-Sussex* (The Oakwood Press, 1975)
Hamilton-Ellis, C., *The London Brighton and South Coast Railway* (Ian Allan, London, 1960)
Mitchell, V. and Smith, K., *Branch Lines to Horsham* (Middleton Press, Midhurst, 1982)

Chapter Three, Henfield at Work
Beswick, M., *Brickmaking in Sussex—A History and Gazetteer* (Middleton Press, Midhurst)
*Cox, D.H., 'William Cooper, millwright and engineers 1828-1876', *Sussex Industrial History, 20* (1990), 2-14
Kelly's Post Office Directory (1838, 1845, 1851, 1855, 1858, 1859, 1862, 1866, 1867, 1874, 1878, 1882, 1887, 1890, 1895, 1899, 1903, 1905, 1907, 1909, 1911, 1913, 1915, 1922, 1927, 1930, 1934, 1938): Henfield
Pigot Directory (1828, 1832, 1838, 1839): Henfield
Stidder, D. and Smith, C., *Watermills of Sussex. Volume II West Sussex* (Pheasant Communications Ltd, 2001)
Waugh, M., *Smuggling in Kent and Sussex 1700-1840* (Countryside Books, Newbury, Berkshire, 1985)

Chapter Four, The Heart of Henfield
Caffyn, J., 'Sussex Schools in the 18th century'. *Sussex Records Society* (1998)
Haylett, A., 'A celebration of 50 years of the N.H.S. General Practice', *Newsletter of the Friends of Henfield Medical Practice* (1998)
Henfield Fire Brigade: Scrapbook
Henfield National School for Boys: Log books, 1868-1889
Henfield National School for Girls: Log books, 1882-1953
Henfield National School for Infants: Log books, 1867-1912
*Henfield National School for Boys: School Register Volume II, 1815-1825
*Henfield Parish Council, 'Financial statements for the years ending 31 March 1896-1935, 1938, 1944, 1946'
*Henfield Parish Council, 'Lamplighter's wages receipt book, 19 August 1911-27 August 1932'

*Henfield Society for Educating the Children of the Poor, 'Minutes of the Proceedings Volume II: August 1815-August 1825'
*Oliver, B., *St Peter's Parish Church, Henfield* (1987)
*Porter, V., *The Village Parliaments* (Phillimore, Chichester, 1994)
*Sayers, D. and Sayers, B., *Henfield Evangelical Free Church Hall* (1998)

Chapter Five, Henfield at War
*Bishop, L., *Henfield in Battledress* (Lucie Bishop, Henfield, 1947)
*Hodgson, B.J., *Record of the Second Volunteer Battalion, Royal Sussex Regiment from 1859-1903* (1903)
*Protestation commanded by the Commons House of Parliament (1641)
*Survey of the Manor of Stretham, Henfield (1647)

Chapter Six, The People of Henfield
*Dame Elizabeth Gresham Charity: Deed of Foundation (1661)
*Dame Elizabeth Gresham Charity: Charity Conveyances (1688)
*Dowson, M.E., Biographical notes in *The Roadmender and other writings*, ed. G.F. Maine (1950)
*Fairless, M., *The Roadmender and other writings* (New Edition, 1950, ed. G.F. Maine)
*Leigh, L., *The Roadmender Country* (The Homeland Associations, Ltd, London, 1923)
*Lower, M.A., 'William Borrer' in *Worthies of Sussex* (Lewes, Sussex, 1865)
*Maine, G.F., 'Roadmender Country' in *The Roadmender and other writings*, ed. G.F. Maine (1950)
*Paterson, L., 'Introduction', in *The Roadmender and other writings*, ed. G.F. Maine (1950)
*Robinson, M., 'William Borrer, botanist', *Sussex County Magazine* (1939)
Seaward, M.R.D., 'Great Discoveries in Bryology and Lichenology: William Borrer (1781-1862), Father of British Lichenology' *The Bryologist* 105, 70-7 (2002)
*Wilberforce, O., *Backsettown, Elizabeth Robins and Octavia Wilberforce* (1952)
*Wolseley, Viscountess, 'Historic houses of Sussex—Backsettown, Henfield', *Country Life*, March 1931

Chapter Seven, Henfield at Leisure
*Henfield Women's Institute: Scrap books and albums
*Squire, H.F. and Squire, A.P., *Henfield Cricket and its Sussex Cradle* (Combridges, Hove, 1949)
*Squire, H.F. and Squire, A.P., *Pre-Victorian Sussex Cricket* (Ditchling Press, Sussex, 1951)

Index

Page numbers in **bold** refer to illustrations or their captions

Adur, River, 1, **1**, 3, 17, 25, 26, **21**, **25-6**, **26**, **32-3**, 35, 36, 57, 85, 104, 134
Allen-Brown, Misses A. & D., 41
Angling clubs, 134, **134**
Anglo-Saxon peoples, 1, 2, 4, **5**, 6, **6**
A.R.P. wardens, 90
Arundel, 77, 78
Assembly Rooms, the, **64**, 65, 74, 75, 84, 89, 91, 111, 124, 132, 133, 136

Backsettown, 4, 12, 82, 90, 103-4, **103**
Baden-Powell Guild, 94, **129**
Badminton, 124
Baigent, Alfred, 49, **51**, **86**, 125
Baigents, builders, 49, 50, **51**
Bailey, James, 56
Baker family, 77, 86, **86**
Bakers, 108-9
Bank House, 108
Barber, Margaret Fairless, 104-5, **105**
Barringer's Mill, 45
Barrow Hill, 2, 4, 13, 78, 101, **101**
Barrow Hill farmhouse, **12**
Barrow Hill House, 41, 45, 90, 98, 100, **100**
Barry, the Rev. P.M., 132
Bartlet, Thomas, 95
Basket Makers Cottages, **52-3**, 56
Batts, 78
Baxter, Allan, 71-2, **73**
Bay Bridge, 25
Baybridge Canal Company, 25, **25**
'Beachcomber', 108
Bedwell, Patricia, 68
Beechings, 29
Beehive Brewery, 53
Belcher family, 95

Bellingham, Thomas, 78
Belson family, 95
Betchley family, 49, 90
Betley, 10, 25, 78, 85
Bignell family, 53
Bineham Bridge, 17, 25, 36
Bines Bridge, 25-6
Bishop, John Terry, 49, 82
Bishop, Lucie, **74**, 75, **76**, **92**, **137**
Blackburne-Hall, Annette, 101
Blackgate Lane, **56**, 59
Blacksmiths, 47-8, **47-8**, **50**
Blackstone, 17, 60
Block, Cdr., 88
Boer Wars, the, 81, 126
Bond, Freda, 107
Boniface, Edward, 77
Borrer family, 20, **24**, 41, 98, 100-1
Borrer, Dawson, 100, **101**
Borrer, Fanny, 101
Borrer, William, 56-7, 62, 64, 71, 98, **99-100**, 100, 126
Botting family, 43-4
Bottings Farm, 13, 26, 104
Bowden family, **88**, 111
Bowler family, **52**, **105**
Bowling, 125, **125**
Bramber, 7, 19
Braose, William de, 7
Brazier, George, **47**
Brazier, John, 48
Brazier, John Albert, 48, **49**, 72, **73**
Breweries, 53
Brick House, 108, 112
Brickworks, 31-2, **32-3**
Bridger family, 95

Brighton, 19, 20, 26-7, 29, 37, 81, 104
British Legion, the, **85**, 136
Broadmere Common, 31, **32**, **52-3**, 56, 70
Broadmere Farm, 56
Brook House, 109
Brookside Farm, 17, **36**
Broomfield Road, **19**
Broomfields, 65, **65**, **80**, 124
Bronze-Age peoples, 2
Browning family, 38, **39**, **51**, **86**, **88**, 131, **131**
Buckwish, 10, 44, 78
Bylsborough, 12
Bysshopp family, 57-8, 71
Bysshopp, Henry, 58, 77-8, **78**, 97, **97**
Bysshopp, Thomas, 12, 58

Cagefoot Lane, 13, 61, 66, 78, 88, **91**, 94, 98,
  127, 136
Canadian soldiers, 90
Canon family, 77
Catsfold, 13
Catsland, 10, 78
Caudle, Dr Adolphus, 65
Caudle, Dr Adolphus William Wisden, 65, 80
Cedar Way, 13, **100**
Celtic peoples, 3-4
Chaete family, 77, 95
Chanctonbury Rural District Council, 29, 70, 72,
  90, 92
Chanctonbury View, 15
Charles I, King, 77-9
Charles II, King, 97
Chatfields, **12**, 101
Chess Brook Green, 15
Chess Brook, the, 35, 43, 134
Chestham Park, 41, **42**, 100, 108
Chichester, bishops of, 7, 8-10, 34, 78-9, 97
Churcher family, 61
Church Lane, 64
Church Street, 13, 23, 34, 102, 106-8
Cibses, 27
Clock House, 56, 111
Collis, Cornelius, 64
Commercial Buildings, 32, 115, **117**
Comrades of the Great War Club, **85**, 134, 136
Congreve, Ambrose, 32
Cook, Fred, 65
Cooper family, 95
Cooper, William, 45
Coopers Way, 75

Coopers Yard, 45, **46**, 47, 75
Council houses, 50, 85, **86**, 92, **93**
Cramp family, 56
Cricket, 90, **116**, 119, **120**
Croft House, 30, **30**, 126, **137**
Croft Lane, 61
Cruttendens, bakers, 66, 108-9, **109**
Cruttenden family, **82**, 108-9, **109**
Curzon, Rt Hon. Robert, 41

Dagbrook Lane, 17
Daisy Croft, the, 15, 50, 120
Darby and Joan Club, **138**
Davy family, 77
Dears, 13
Deer Park, 9, 15
Dixon-Brown, Ethel & Hilda, 129-30, **130**
Domesday Book, 7-8, 41, 43
Downes, Col. John, M.P., 78-9
Dropping Holms, 13, 17, **18**, 43
Dunfords, bakers, 108
Dunlop, the Rev. Charles, 101, 135
'Dykes', 90, 107, **107**

Eardley Hall Memorial Institute, 58, 65, 90, 120,
  123, **135**, 136
East Martyns, 107
Eastout, 10, 31
Eatons Farm, 13, 25, 78, 98
Elm Lodge, 80, 112
Elvins, Fr. Mark, 71
Emett, Rowland, 108, **108**
English Civil War, the, 77-9

Fabians Way, 50
Faircox Lane, 10, 27, 85
'Fairless, Michael', 104-5
Faith, Adam, 108
Farrell, Alfred, 49
Fishing clubs, 134
Flower Farm Close, 50
Football, 58, 92, **93**, 119-122, **121**
Forges Cottage, 61
Frankwell, Elnor, 95
Freeman, Jean, 123
Frogshole, 118
Funnell family, 111, **111**
Furners Farm, 38, 86
Furners Lane, 2, 12-3, 17, 23, **24**, 43, **91**
Furners Mead, 50, 81, 125

Gallop, Nicholas, 77, 95
Gander, Alf, 50
Gander family, **73**
George V, King, 70
George field, the, **50**, 120, 140
George Hotel, The, **18**, 20, 29, **39**, 72, 86, 90, 120, 126
George, Prince of Wales, 19-20
Gillett, 'Joe', 72, **73**, **74**, 76
Girls' Friendly Society, the, 90, **128**
'G.I.s', 90
Glasby, Barbara & Dulcima, 105-6, **106**
Goacher, Bill, **89**, **117**, 118
Godley, William, 62, 64
Goffe family, 77, 95
Golden Square, 20, 45, 48, 61, 72, 87, 101, 125, **132-3**
Goldsmith, John, 77
Gordon, Brig. Gen. J.R.P., 81
Gratwick, John, 98
Gray, John & Rosa, 106
Great War, the, 82-4, **82-5**
Greenfield family, 32, 38, **38-9**, 53, 75, 77, 95
Greensand Way, the, 4, 10
Gresham Charity, 97-8
Gresham, Dame Elizabeth, 97-8
Gresham Place, 27
Grey House, the, 61
Grinstead Lane, 17, 98
Guides, Girl, 129-31

Haine family, 95
Hamfelde, 1
Hall, Eardley N., 20, **24**, 100
Hall, Elizabeth, 98
Hall family, 20, 41, 98-101
Hall, George, 59
Hall, John Eardley, **44**, 45, 71, 101, 136
Hall, Nathaniel, **23**
Harcourt-Vernon, Misses, 88
Hay Croft, 66, 88
Hayne family, 77
Heavers family, 38
Henfield and District Ambulance Club, 72
Henfield and District Lions Club, 94
Henfield and District Sports Centre, 70
Henfield Assembly Rooms Company, 74-5
Henfield Benefit Association for Nursing the Sick, 66-7
Henfield Choral & Operatic Society, 132-3

Henfield Chrysanthemum, Dahlia and Horticultural Society, 126
Henfield Common, 2, 4, 34, 37-8, 41, 45, 53, 63-4, 70, 78, 82, 84, 86, 92, **93**, 107, **116**, 119, 120, 122-3, **122**, 125-6, 130, 136, 138, **139**, 140
Henfield Cricket Club, 119
Henfield Evangelical Free Church, 58-9, **58**, **96**, 112
Henfield Fire Brigade, 71-2, **71**, **73**
Henfield Flower Club, 126
Henfield Football Club, 119-22, **121**
Henfield Gas and Coke Company, **54-6**, 56
Henfield Lodge, **42**, 61
Henfield Medical Centre, 68
Henfield Motors, 72
Henfield Museum, 2, 26, 56, 72, 75-6
Henfield Parish Council, 56, 68-72, **69**, 74-76, **74**, 92, 124
Henfield Place, 12, **14**, 23, 60, 70, 88, 98, 123, **128**
Henfield Players, the, 89, 133
Henfield railway station, **27**, **28**
Henfield Tavern, the, 53
Henfield Tennis Club, 123-4
Henfield Village Hall, 75-6, 133
Henfield Village Produce Association, 88, 126, **127**
Henfield and Woodmancote Home Guard, 86-7, **87**, 89-90
Henfield Women's Institute, 75, 82, **83**, 87-8, 136-7, **137**
Henfield Young Farmers' Club, **131**
Hewitts, 49, 68
High Street, the, 8, 13, 15, **15**, 17, 23, 32, 34, 37, 41, 45, **46**, 48, **48**, **50**, 53, 56, 58-9, 61, 65, 71, 74, 78, 79-80, **82-91**, 90, 94, 106, 108-115, **109-14**, **126-27**, 129, 135-6, **135**, **137**, 140
Hillman family, **110**, 111, **115**
Hills family, 38, 77
Hobbs, Arthur, 49
Hobbs, Brenda, 71
Hobbs family, 95
Hockey, 92, 122-3
Hoe Wood, 9, 35
Holden family, 77, 133
Holder family, **42**, **118**
Holedean Farm, 10, 13, 38
Holkham family, 48
Hollands Lane, 7, 10, 13, 17, 44, **54-5**, 85
Hollands Road, 50, 85, **86**

Holmwood, 65, **66**
Holney family, 77, 98
Holt, Dr Arthur, 65, 67, **66**
Horn Lane, 4
Horsham District Council, 70
Hughes family, **52**
Hulbert, Edith, 64
Hundred Steddle, 6, 37, 70
Hundred, the, 107

'Imps', the, 89, **132-3**, 133-4
Iron-Age peoples, 3-4

Jasmine House, 111
Jennings, Alfred, 48
Junior Imperial League, 89, **132-3**, 133-4
Jupp family, 77, 95, 131

Kenwellmersh, Ann, **13**
Kindersley, 37, 98, **99**
Kindersley Trust, the, 98
Kings Field, the, 70, 123-4, **124**
Knowles, Miss, 70, 84

Lashmars Hall, 10, **11**, 78
Lavender Cottage, **40**, 41
Lea, Canon R.J., 119, 123, 138, **139**
Leeches, 26
Legg family, 95
Lelliott family, 26
Lewis, Dr Charles, 65-6, 74, **80**
Lewis, Dr Frederick, **44**, 65
Library, public, **64**, 65
Lidbetter, George, 49
Lipride, 31, 78
Littler, Prince, 108
Little Whaphams, 61
London, Brighton & South Coast Railway, 27, 29
London House, 56, 111
London Road, 13, 53
Longley Brothers, 79, 108
Longley, Henry, 74, 108
Lydds, the, **44**, 45, 90

Malthouse Cottage, 53
Manor Way, 13, 50
Manor Close, 13, 50
Martin, Ebenezer, 59
Martyn Lodge, 41, 90, 102, **102**, 129, **130**
Martyns Close, 50

Mercer family, 95
Mesolithic peoples, *2*
Miles, Alan, 48
Miles, Harold, 48
Miles, Tom, 48, **48**
Mill Drive, 13, **100**
Millfield, 84
Mills, Eliza, 65
Mills, steam, 45
Mills, water, 41, 43, **43**
Mills, wind, 44-5, **44**
Millwrights, 45, 47
Milne, Malcolm & Hilda, 90, 107, **107**
Mermaid Cottage, 23
Mock Bridge, **21**, 25-7, 70, 104
Mockbridge House, 13, **52**, 104-5, **105**
Moore family, **110**, **137**
Morey, May, 90, **137**
Morgan family, 65
Morley family, 53, 77
Morris family, 112, **112**
Morton, J.B., 108
Moustows Manor, 6, 8, 23, 61, 81
Musson family, **88**, 109, **110**
Muzzell family, 95
Myrtle Villa, 106

Napoleonic Wars, 79, 98
Neale, James, 45
Neolithic peoples, 2, **2**
Nep Town, 2, 8, 13, 17, 37, **44**, 44-5, 48
Nep Town Mission, **59**
Nep Town Road, 13, 23, **24**, 50, **56**, 64, 132, **140**
New Barn Lane, 97
New Hall, 4, 12, 23, **23**, 27, 34, 41, 78, 98
New Hall Lane, 88
New Inn, 17, 25, **26**, 37
Norman peoples, 7-8
Norton House, 98

O'Brien, the Rev. John, 80
Old Bell Inn, the, 53, 120
Oliver, Barbara, Lady, 137
Oreham Common, 70
Oreham Manor, 8, 10

Page family, 77, 95
Pakyns Manor, Hurstpierpoint, 98
Palaeolithic peoples, 2
Parham Park, 41, 57, 97

Parish relief, 36, **37**
Parish Rooms, the, **138**
Park Farm, 89
Park Road, 30, 86
Parsonage House, 12, 57, 77-8, **78**, 97
Parsonage Farm, 9, 15, 27, 34-5, 50, 68
Parsons family, 38, **73**, 77, **93**, **116**
Partridge Green, 29, 84
Pattenden family, **22**, 111, **117**, **120**
Pattenden, R., 31
Paynesfield, 89
Penny, R.H., 32
Pinchnose Green, 34, 118
Plough Inn, the, 48, 82, 88, 121
Pokerlee, 10, 78
Pools, the, 31, 90
Potwell, 10, 61, 78, 98, 122
Powell, William, 30, **46**, 48, **71**, 76
Pratt, Dr Eldon, 65
'Prefab' houses, 59, 92, **93**
Prisoners of war, 84, 90, 92

Quoits, 122, **122**

Railways, 26-30, **27-8**
Rainbow Coffee Tavern, 135-6, **135**
Rainsford, George, 78
Rainsford, Meneleb, **13**
Rainsford, Prosper, 12, 78
Redbarn Cottages, 58
Red Oaks, 60, 101
Rehoboth Baptist Chapel, 59-60, **60**
Robins, Elizabeth, 102-4, **103**, 136
Roman Catholic Church of Corpus Christi, 60-1, **60**, 71
Roman peoples, 4, **4**
Rothery field, 2, **37**, 86, 122
Royal Observer Corps, 86
Ruff, Rolf, 115
Rus House, **50**, 112
Rye Farm, 13, 43, 118

St Anthony's Cottage, **8**, 53
St Hugh's, Charterhouse, 34
St John Ambulance Brigade, 72, 116
St Peter's Church House, 57
St Peter's Church of England School, 62-5, **62-3**
St Peter's Parish Church, 4-6, 34, 57-8, **57**, 62, 71, 89, 100, 111
St Peter's Parish Room, 57, 65, 89, **138**

Sandy Lane, 27, 32, **33**, 123
School, Boys', 62-5, **62**, 76, 89, 127
School, Girls' 63-4, **63**
School, Infants', **63**, 64, 132
Schools, private, 61, **61**
Scouts, Boy, 126-9, **128-9**
Scutt family, 81
Second World War, the, 45, 67, 85-92, **87-93**, 101, 104
Selsey, bishops of, 6-7
Shepherd, Ron, **116**, 118, 121
Shermanbury, 88, 104
Shermanbury Grange, 26-7
Shermanbury Place, 104
Shiprods, 12, 45, 98
Shoreham, 7, 17, 19, 29, 36, 82, 101
Shoreham Road, 35
Skilton family, **92**, **118**, **121**
Smith family, 95
Smuggling, 36-7
South Downs, 1-3, 41, 104
South View Terrace, 4, **16**, 32, 85
Springhills, **87**, **101**
Squire, Dorothy, 87
Squire, Dr Henry, 65-7, 72, **92**, 124
Squire, Dr John, 67, **74**, **76**
Squire, Harold, 107
Stained glass, 58, 105-6
Standen, Alice, 75, **83**, 134
Standen family, 38
Stapleton, Thomas, 97, **97**
Staples Barn Farm, 34, 78, 131
Station Road, 13, 15
Station Road, Lower, 13, 45, 98
Station Road, Upper, 15, 37, 61, 70, 85, 98, **99**, 105
Stern, Lilian, 60
Stevens, Thomas, 56
Stonepit Lane, 34, 86
Stenning family, 95
Steyning, 7, 29, 34, 64
Stokes family, 77, 95
Stoolball, 58, 123
Stretham Bridge, 85, 88
Stretham, manor of, 4, 6-9, 41, 44, 78, 97
Stretham Manor, 4, 8, **10**, 27, 34, 78, 97
Stretham, moated site, 4, **9**
Sunnyside, 105
Sussex Rifle Volunteers, 76, 79-81, **80**
Sussex Wildlife Trust, 43

Sussex Yeomanry and Territorial Army, 81, **81**
Swains Farm, 13, 38
Swingler, Sgt W., 81-2

Tanyard, the, 34, **35**, 70, **117**, 118, **123**
Tennis, 123-4, **124**
Terry's Cross, 68
Thorns, David, 90
Thorns family, **73**, 111, **113**, **118**, 119
Tipnoak, Hundred of, 6
Tipnoak Women's Institute, 137
Tobitt, Charles, **26**, 45, 59, 71, 112, **113**
Tobitt family, 112, **112**
Tompsett family, **109**, **110**
Turnpike trusts, 19, **20-1**
Tyler, Charles & Mary, 112, **114-15**, 115, **120**

Upper Beeding, 6, 19

Vanderbilt's stage coach, **22**, 82
Vicarage, the, **139**
Victoria, Queen, 29, 58
Village Hall, the, 47, 75-6
Vinall family, 44, 49, 77, 95
Vinalls, builders, 50, **51**, **140**
Violet Nursery, the, **40**, 41, **122**

Wade, Audrey, 126-7
Wade, Charles, 74, 126
Wade, Major A.G., 126-7
Wakeford, the Rev. W., 138
Wantley Farm, 34
Wantley Manor, **9**, 124
Wantley, manor of, 8, 43
Wantley, New, 50, 92, **93**
Wantley, Old, 92
Warbald, Earl, 4, 6
Ward family, 49, 53
War memorials, the, **85**, 92, **93**, 94
Weald Clay, 1, 31
Wealden iron industry, 3, 13

West End Lane, 17, 23, 35, 37, 85, 92, 118
West family, 20
West, Henry T., **24**, 68, 80
West Grinstead, 25
West Mill, 43
West Sussex County Council, 29, 65, 67, 72
Wheelwrights, 49
White family, 38, 77, **88**, 95
White Hart Inn, the, 20, **22**, 23, 34, **79**
White House, the, **61**, **139**
Whiting, Peggy, 131
Whiting, the Rev., 59
Whittome, Donald, 38, **74**
Whittome, Eric, 38, **74**, 75, **76**
Wilberforce, Dr Octavia, 103-4
Williamson, Hardie & Susan, 106, **106**
Windmill Lane, 17, 32, 37
Wisden, Charles, **24**, 56
Wisden, Thomas, 20, **24**, 41
Wisden, William, 34
Wood, Albert, 59
Wood, John, 41, **42**
Wood, Lucretia, 41, **42**, 100
Woodard, Nathaniel, 81, 101-2
Woodard schools, 101-2
Woodard, William, 81
Woodlawn, 67, **68**
Woodmancote, 6, 12
Woods Mill, 4, 35, 43, **43**, 45, 89
Woolgar family, 95-6, **96**, **128**
Woolgar, Harry, 96
Woolgar, John, 95, 97
Woolgar, Mary, 48, 95
Woolgar, Private, 81
Woolgar, Thomas, 95-6
Woolgar, William, 77, 56
Wooller, Nurse, 67, **67**, **138**, **140**
Woolley, Sir Leonard, **23**
Wright, S.G., 91

Youth clubs, 132